THE MODERN LIBRARY
OF THE WORLD'S BEST BOOKS

THE COMPLEAT ANGLER

*The publishers will be pleased to send, upon request, an
illustrated folder setting forth the purpose and scope of*
THE MODERN LIBRARY, *and listing each volume
in the series. Every reader of books will find titles he has
been looking for, handsomely printed, in unabridged
editions, and at an unusually low price.*

THE COMPLEAT ANGLER

BY

IZAAK WALTON

THE MODERN LIBRARY · NEW YORK

Random House IS THE PUBLISHER OF

THE MODERN LIBRARY

BENNETT A. CERF · DONALD S. KLOPFER · ROBERT K. HAAS

Manufactured in the United States of America

Printed by Parkway Printing Company   Bound by H. Wolff

TABLE OF CONTENTS

THE COMPLEAT ANGLER

THE LIFE OF IZAAK WALTON

IZAAK WALTON, the loving biographer of several of
his friends, has left little record of the details of his
own life. One of his favourite mottoes, "Study to be
quiet", was exemplified in his long and apparently un-
eventful existence. Could he but have written his own
biography, it had abounded with evidences of his
strong humanity, of his appreciation of the small things
of life, of the value he set upon friendship and human
relationships. All this may be inferred from his writ-
ings, but a brief account of the main facts of his life as
they are known is needed to form a setting for his per-
sonality.

Walton was born at Stafford on August 9, 1593. He
was baptised in the Church of St. Mary on September
21, and according to the entry on the register he was
the son of Jervis Walton, of whom nothing further is
known except that he died in February 1596/7. Of
Walton's mother nothing is known, not even her name.
His early life and education was presumably conducted
at Stafford, but no certain facts are known until ex-
amination is made of the records of the Ironmongers'
Company, where it is stated that having been "late
apprentice to Thomas Grinsall" he was "admitted and
sworne a free brother of this companie" on 12 Novem-

ber, 1617/18.[1] From this it may be inferred that he had already been for at least seven years in London, and so must have been there in 1611 when he was eighteen. He may even have come sooner than this, for a reference in his will to "my cozen Griensell's widow" shows that he was related to his first employer. His business was formerly believed to have been that of a haberdasher or linen draper, but this is shown to be untrue both by the records already mentioned and by his marriage licence of 1626, in which he is described as "of the City of London, Ironmonger".[2] Whatever his occupation may have been it did not prevent his following his bent, which was a genius for friendship. The ironmonger's apprentice became the intimate associate of many of the most distinguished men of his time, and it is evident that he had unusual attractions of mind and personality. Part of this was no doubt his love of literature, which must have shown itself at an early age. When he was only twenty he was the object of dedicatory verses prefixed to a poem, *The Loves of Amos and Laura*, by S. P., 1613. The writer, who addresses Walton as "thou thrice beloved friend", may have been Samuel Purchas, author of *The Pilgrimes*, but this is uncertain. He attributes to Walton some of the responsibility for the composition of the poem.

Walton carried on his business in Chancery Lane and Fleet Street, and he is stated to have lived in 1624 on the north side of Fleet Street in a house two doors

---

[1] See *Notes and Queries*, Dec. 29, 1928.
[2] *Ibid.*

west of the end of Chancery Lane. From 1628 to 1644 he probably lived in Chancery Lane itself, and the parish books of St. Dunstan's show that he fulfilled the ordinary duties of a householder as scavenger, juryman, constable, grand juryman, overseer of the poor, sidesman and vestryman.[1] He is also stated to have served as a "gentleman in foins" in the mayoralty of Sir Thomas Campbell, and to have been chosen Warden of the Yeomanry in 1637.[2] It may be supposed that it was his residence in Fleet Street that led him to attend services at St. Dunstan's in the West, and so to the friendship of Dr. Donne, who was Vicar of St. Dunstan's from 1621. He also came to know others of Donne's circle, such as Sir Henry Wotton, Dr. Henry King, afterwards Bishop of Chichester, and John Hales of Eton. George Herbert he had met, but the acquaintance was so slight that he did not claim him as a friend. Other literary friends, however, are mentioned in his writings, such as Ben Jonson and Michael Drayton, and it is evident that he might even have known Shakespeare, though of this he has given no sign.

His first marriage took place on December 27, 1626, his wife being Rachel Floud of Canterbury, through whom he became connected with the Cranmer family. Their marriage chest, now preserved at Warwick Castle, carries on it two punning lines, which may be Walton's earliest surviving composition. Rachel Walton lived for nearly fourteen years after her marriage

[1] *The Complete Angler*, ed. Nicolas, 1836, p. clix.
[2] *The Complete Angler*, ed. Marston, Oxford, 1921, p. xii.

and bore six children, but none of them survived infancy. Nothing further is known of Walton's married life. Rachel Walton died in 1640, and six years later Walton married for the second time, his wife being Anne Ken, half-sister to Bishop Ken of Winchester. By her he had three children, a daughter and two sons, one of whom survived. Anne Walton lived for sixteen years after her marriage, dying at Worcester in 1662, probably while she and her husband were with their friend George Morley, then Bishop of Worcester, who is known to have made Walton his steward.[1] She was buried in the Cathedral, where her monument carries the epitaph printed here among Walton's Miscellaneous Writings.

Meanwhile, in 1644, Walton had left his house in Chancery Lane, because it was "dangerous for honest men to be there", dangerous, that is, for a Royalist. There is no reason, however, for supposing that he left London, and it is probable that in 1650 he was living in Clerkenwell. In 1651 he played a small part in the Commonwealth drama, helping to restore to King Charles a ring, the "lesser George", saved from some baggage which had been captured by Cromwell after the battle of Worcester. Walton did not want high adventure, but sought rather the contemplative man's recreation. It was in the pursuit of angling that his spirit found its greatest satisfaction, and it is certain that Walton lost no opportunity of indulging this fancy.

[1] See an article by John Beresford in *Notes and Queries*, Sept. 15, 1923 (13 s., p. 204). The fact was ascertained by Canon Price.

He delighted particularly in fishing the river Lea in the neighbourhood of Ware. He also paid visits to Stafford and acquired a house and land near the town at Shallowford. The house, which is still standing, may actually have been his birthplace, but whether or not he had this reason for acquiring it, it certainly gave him further opportunity of pursuing his grand passion in a type of stream different from those of his London haunts.

As he grew older, he became intimate with an increasing number of ecclesiastics, among whom were Richard Hooker, Robert Sanderson, Thomas Fuller and George Morley. These names have survived, but it cannot be doubted that Walton's love of fishing brought him many other friends, obscurer, though equally dear. The same influence cemented one distinguished friendship, Charles Cotton, the poet, forming with Walton the most famous piscatorial association in history. Charles Cotton the elder, of Beresford Hall on the borders of Staffordshire and Derbyshire, was the friend of Wotton, Donne and Walton, and so his son, the younger Charles, had known Walton from childhood. Walton had published his *Compleat Angler* in 1653, and it had immediately become popular, so that several editions were sold in a few years. The author had spent many a quiet happy day fishing with worm or fly in the rivers round London or in Dovedale, and the result was the most engaging treatise on angling ever written. It may not be impeccable in scientific accuracy, and a great deal of it is not connected with fishing, but the book was the product of long contentment and repose, and reflects its writer's character as clearly as the stillest pool ever gave back his face. Walton's association with the worldly Charles Cotton may seem somewhat incongruous, yet Cotton's continuation, or imitation, of *The Compleat Angler,* with its letter addressed to his "Father" Izaak Walton, has had more part in keeping his fame bright than any of his other writings. The two books were first printed together in 1676, and have scarcely ever been divorced through innumerable editions until the present day. *The Compleat Angler* possesses an innocent charm which no amount of petting from Walton's devotees can spoil; yet it is safe to assert that the artlessness with which it was composed is more apparent than real. Walton was a more practised writer than he allowed the ordinary reader to discern; though at what date he first began to write, it is now impossible to guess. His earliest published work was his elegy on Donne, included in the first edition of *Poems by* J. D. in 1633. During the remainder of his life he wrote at intervals elegies, epitaphs, commendatory verses, and prefaces for various works, an account of which will be found in the notes on the Miscellaneous Writings. His biographical faculty he first began to exercise in 1639. He had before this been collecting material for Sir Henry Wotton with which to write an account of Donne's life, but Wotton died in 1639 without having carried out his intention, whereupon Walton stepped into the gap, and composed the celebrated Life printed with Donne's Sermons in 1640. Donne had been the friend of his youth and was one of the most extraordinary figures of his time, so that Walton was unlikely ever to find again so inspiriting a subject. Yet the later Lives of Wotton, Herbert, Hooker and Sanderson[1] possess almost the same grace and spontaneity, even when Walton had never seen the subject of his study. He understood something of the artistic value of small details and personal traits, and so was the forerunner of the most modern exponents of the art of biography.

By 1662 Walton was nearly seventy years of age, but this did not deter him from obtaining from the Bishop of London a forty years' lease of a house in Paternoster Row; nor from asking, in 1670, for an extension of the lease on condition of his rebuilding the house, which had been burnt down in the Great Fire. Evidently his vigour was still considerable, though in the course of nature it gradually abated during the last twenty years of his life. He was fortunate in possessing a loyal friend and a loving daughter, so that his old age was made happy and comfortable by the division of his time between these two. The friend was George Morley, whom Walton had first known as a canon and Dean of Christ Church, Oxford, afterwards as Bishop of Worcester, and finally as Bishop of Win-

---

[1] He also collected materials for a Life of John Hales of Eton, and his notes are printed here among the Miscellaneous Writings, but these were not used as far as is known.

chester. Morley had actually appointed Walton as his steward, when he was at Worcester and probably also at Winchester, so that much of his old age was spent in retreat at Farnham Castle, the episcopal residence. Many of his books were kept there, and it was at Morley's suggestion that he wrote the last three of his Lives. He was further attracted to Winchester because his daughter Anne had married Dr. Hawkins, who was Prebendary of Winchester and Rector of Droxford, a village situated twelve miles from the city. Recent investigations[1] have shown that Walton spent much of his last years at Droxford, and that several of the friends mentioned in his will lived there.

In 1680, when he was eighty-seven, he published another work, *Love and Truth,* consisting of two letters purporting to have been written to a citizen of Coventry in 1657 and 1679. The tract is concerned with church observance, religion and politics, and was not acknowledged by Walton. The evidence of authorship, discussed in the notes that follow, was, however, too strong to be put aside, and the work has here been admitted to the canon of Walton's complete writings. A vein of piety can be discerned in all his work, and became more obvious the older he grew. *Love and Truth* has fewer attractions than anything else he wrote, but there is nothing in it that is inconsistent with his character and beliefs.

---

[1] See *The Wild Flowers of Selborne and other Papers,* by the Rev. John Vaughan, Rector of Droxford and Hon. Canon of Winchester, London, 1906, pp. 157-171.

It does not seem to have occurred to Walton before 1683 that he might die, but at last, on August 9 of that year, his ninetieth birthday, he decided to make his will, the text of which is given here among his Miscellaneous Writings. He disposed of his London property in Paternoster Row and Chancery Lane, of land which he had acquired near Winchester, and of his Staffordshire estate, the income from which was to be applied, after his son's interest had lapsed, to charitable purposes in the town of Stafford. His books at Winchester and Droxford were left, except for a few special bequests, to his daughter; to his son he left those at Farnham Castle, and some of these are to be found at the present time in Salisbury Cathedral Library, the younger Izaak having afterwards become a Canon of Salisbury. Friends and servants were not forgotten, and finally a long list of names is given of other friends and relations who were to receive at his death mourning rings with the motto: "A friend's farewell. I. W. obiet". A special ring was to be given to Bishop Morley with the motto: "A mite for a million". Izaak Walton in his ninetieth year was "in perfect memory", and characteristically determined that as many of his human ties as possible should be kept intact even after his bodily presence had passed away. The will was signed on August 16, 1683, and the intentions expressed in it were soon to be realised, for on December 15 of the same year, during a severe frost, he died in the house of his son-in-law in the Close at Winchester.

He was buried without ostentation in Prior Silkstead's Chapel in the Cathedral.

Izaak Walton's appearance in later life has been recorded in the portrait by Jacob Huysman,[1] from which the copper-plate in the present work has been engraved, and in the pastel by Edmund Ashfield.[2] These pictures represent a man of quiet and benevolent demeanour, whose semi-clerical dress is perhaps to be attributed to his office as steward to Bishop Morley. It is quite evident that Walton was no mere toady to the great, but that his transparently honest character was loved for its own sake. He also showed some particularity in the choice of his friends, for Charles Cotton observes that "my father Walton will be seen twice in no man's company he does not like, and likes none but such as he believes to be very honest men". Had he been the friend and biographer of Donne alone, that fact had been the proof of his worth, for Donne's powerful mind would not have suffered the attentions of a fool or a charlatan. The terms on which he stood with Sir Henry Wotton and the rest would clinch the matter if further evidence were needed.

Walton's own spirit he has himself sketched while describing the death of his friend, Robert Sanderson: "Thus this pattern of meekness and primitive innocence changed this for a better life. 'Tis now too late to wish that my life may be like his; for I am in the

---

[1] In the National Portrait Gallery.
[2] Now in the possession of Dr. Samuel Lambert of New York.

eighty-fifth year of my age; but I beseech Almighty God that my death may; and do as earnestly beg of every reader to say Amen. *Blessed is the man in whose spirit there is no guile* (Ps. xxxii. 2)."

GEOFFREY KEYNES.

BIBLIOGRAPHICAL NOTE

WALTON's treatise on fishing was printed five times in the seventeenth century. It was *first* published in 1653 with an engraved title-page and engravings of six fishes in the text. The *second* edition of 1655 contains many alterations and additions to the text, the number of pages being increased from 246 to 355, and the number of chapters from 13 to 21. Seven commendatory poems were prefixed. Four engravings of fishes were added. The *third* edition was printed in 1661 and re-issued in 1664, with a new title-page. A commendatory poem by Brome previously printed is omitted, and there are a few alterations in the text. The most considerable additions are the "Postscript touching the Lawes of Angling" and the Index. The *fourth* edition was printed in 1668 and closely followed the third. The *fifth* edition, printed in 1676, introduced further changes. The text was revised and minor alterations made throughout. Considerable additions were also made, the length of the text being increased by 20 pages. The copper-plates were re-engraved. Further, the Second Part by Charles Cotton was added for the first time. Sometimes the sheets were bound up with a third work, the fourth edition of *The Experi-*

enc'd Angler by Colonel Robert Venables, a general title-page, *The Universal Angler,* being prefixed to the whole.

The Compleat Angler was reprinted 10 times in the eighteenth century, about 117 times in the nineteenth century, and between 30 and 40 times in the twentieth century. Of a single edition published by Cassell & Co. in 1886, 80,000 copies had been sold by 1914. The text of the fifth edition, 1676, has usually been followed, and the principal editors have been Moses Browne (1750), Sir John Hawkins (1760), John Major (1823), Sir Harris Nicolas (1836), Bethune (1847), R. B. Marston (1888), and R. le Gallienne (1897).

In the present volume the text has been taken from the fourth edition of 1668.

To *the* Right Worshipful
JOHN OFFLEY *of* Madely
Manor in the County of Stafford
Esq.: My Most Honoured
FRIEND

SIR,

I HAVE made so ill use of your former favours, as by them to be encouraged to intreat that they may be enlarged to the *patronage* and *protection* of this Book; and I have put on a modest confidence, that I shall not be deny'd, because it is a Discourse of F*ish* and F*ishing,* which you know so well, and both love and practise so much.

You are assured (though there be ignorant men of another belief) that A*ngling* is an A*rt;* and you know that A*rt* better than others; and, that this is truth is demonstrated by the fruits of that pleasant labour which you enjoy when you purpose to give rest to your mind, and divest your self of your more serious business, and (which is often) dedicate a day or two to this R*ecreation.*

At which time, if *common Anglers* should attend you, and be eye witnesses of the success, not of your *fortune* but your *skill,* it would doubtless beget in them an emulation to be like you, and that emulation might beget an industrious diligence to be so: but I know it is not attainable by common capacities. And there be

17

now many men of great *wisdom, learning,* and *experience,* that love and practise this *Art,* that know I speak the truth.

Sir, This pleasant curiosity of Fish and Fishing (of which you are so great a Master) has been thought worthy the *pens* and *practises* of divers in other Nations, that have been reputed men of great *learning* and *wisdom,* and amongst those of this Nation, I remember Sir *Henry Wotton* (a dear lover of this Art) has told me that his intentions were to write a Discourse of the Art, and in praise of *Angling,* and doubtless he had done so, if death had not prevented him; the remembrance of which hath often made me sorry, for if he had lived to do it, then the unlearned *Angler* had seen some better Treatise of this Art, a Treatise worthy his perusal, which (though some have undertaken) I could never yet see in English.

But mine may be thought as *weak* and as *unworthy* of common view; and I do here freely confess, that I should rather excuse my self, than censure others, my own Discourse being liable to so many exceptions; against which you (Sir) might make this one, *That it can contribute nothing to your Knowledge.* And lest a longer Epistle may diminish your pleasure, I shall not adventure to make this Epistle any longer than to add this following truth, *That I am really,*

SIR,

Your most affectionate Friend,

and most humble Servant,

Iz. Wa.

To all Readers of this
Discourse but especially to the
HONEST ANGLER

I *think fit to tell thee these following truths, That* I
did neither undertake, *nor* write, *nor* publish, *and
much less* own, *this Discourse to please my self: and
having been too easily drawn to please others, as* I
*propos'd not the gaining of credit by this undertaking,
so I would not willingly lose any part of that to which
I had a just title before I begun it, and therefore desire
and hope, if I deserve not commendation, yet I may
obtain pardon.*

*And though this Discourse may be lyable to some
Exceptions, yet* I *cannot doubt but that most Readers
may receive so much* pleasure or profit *by it, as may
make it worthy the time of their perusal, if they be not
very busie men. And this is all the confidence that* I
*can put on concerning the merit of what is here offered
to their consideration and censure; and if the last prove
too severe, I have a liberty, and am resolv'd to neglect
it.*

And I *wish the* Reader *also to take notice, that in
writing of it* I *have made myself a* recreation *of a rec-*
reation; *and that it might prove so to him, and not
read* dull *and* tediously, I *have in several places mixt*

(*not any scurrility, but*) *some innocent, harmless mirth; of which, if thou be a severe sowre-complexion'd man, then* I *here disallow thee to be a competent judge; for* Divines *say,* There are offences given, and offences not given but taken.

And I *am the willinger to justifie the pleasant part of it, because, though it is known* I *can be serious at seasonable times, yet the whole* Discourse *is, or rather was, a picture of my own disposition, especially in such dayes and times as* I *have laid aside business, and gone a fishing with honest* Nat. *and* R. Roe; *but they are gone, and with them most of my pleasant hours, even as a shadow that passeth away, and returns not.*

Next *let me tell the* Reader, *that in that which is the more useful part of this* Discourse, *that is to say, the observations of the* nature *and* breeding, *and* seasons, *and* catching of fish, I *am not so simple as not to know, that a captious* Reader *may find exceptions against something said of some of these; and therefore* I *must intreat him to consider, that experience teaches us to know, that several* Countries *alter the time, and* I *think almost the manner of fishes breeding, but doubtless of their being in season; as may appear by three* Rivers *in* Monmouthshire, *namely* Severn, Wie, *and* Usk, *where* Cambden (Brit. *f.* 633) *observes, that in the river* Wie, Salmon *are in season from* Sept. *to* April, *and we are certain, that in* Thames *and* Trent, *and in most other Rivers they be in season the six hotter moneths.*

Now *for the Art of* catching *fish, that is to say, how to make a man that was none, to be an* Angler *by a book; he that undertakes it shall undertake a harder task than Mr.* Hales (*a most valiant and excellent Fencer*) *who in a printed book called,* A private School of Defence, *undertook by it to teach that art or science, and was laugh'd at for his labour. Not but that many useful things might be learnt by that book, but he was laugh'd at, because that art was not to be taught by words, but practice: and so must* Angling. *And in this* Discourse *I do not undertake to say all that is known, or may be said of it, but I undertake to acquaint the* Reader *with many things that are not usually known to every* Angler; *and I shall leave gleanings and observations enough to be made out of the experience of all that love and practise this recreation, to which I shall encourage them. For* Angling *may be said to be so like the* Mathematicks, *that it can ne'r be fully learnt; at least not so fully, but that there wil stil be more new experiments left for the trial of other men that succeed us.*

But I *think all that love this game may here learn something that may be worth their money, if they be not poor and needy men; and in case they be, I then wish them to forbear to buy it; for I write not to get money, but for pleasure, and this* Discourse *boasts of no more; for I hate to promise much, and deceive the* Reader.

And *however it proves to him, yet I am sure I have*

found a high content in the search and conference of what is here offer'd to his view and censure: I wish him as much in the perusal of it, and so I might here take my leave, but will stay a little and tell him, that whereas it is said by many, that in flye-fishing for a Trout, *the Angler must observe his twelve several flies for the twelve moneths of the year; I say he that follows that rule, shall be as sure to catch fish, and be as wise as he that makes* Hay *by the fair dayes in an Almanack, and no surer; for those very flyes that use to appear about and on the water in one moneth of the year, may the following year come almost a moneth sooner or later, as the same year proves colder or hotter; and yet in the following* Discourse *I have set down the twelve flyes that are in reputation with many Anglers, and they may serve to give him some light concerning them. And he may note that there is in* Wales, *and other* Countries, *peculiar* flyes, *proper to the particular place or* Country; *and doubtless, unless a man makes a flye to counterfeit that very flye in that place, he is like to lose his labour, or much of it: But for the generality, three or four* flyes *neat and rightly made, and not too big, serve for a* Trout *in most rivers all the* Summer. *And for* Winter *flie-fishing it is as useful as an* Almanack *out of date. And of these (because as no man is born an artist, so no man is born an angler) I thought fit to give thee this notice.*

When I have told the Reader, that in this third Impression there are many enlargements, gathered both by my own observation, *and the communication of* friends, I shall stay him no longer than to wish him a rainy evening to read this following Discourse; *and that* (if he be an honest Angler) the East wind may never blow when he goes a Fishing.

I. W.

COMMENDATORY VERSES

To my dear Brother-in-law Mr. Iz. *Walton*,
upon his *Compleat Angler*.

ERASMUS *in his learned Colloquies*
Has mixt some toyes, that by varieties
He might entice all Readers: for in him
Each child *may wade, or tallest* giant *swim.*
And such is this Discourse: there's none so low,
Or highly learn'd, to whom hence may not flow
Pleasure and information: both which are
Taught us with so much art, that I *might swear*
Safely the choicest Critick cannot tell,
Whether your matchless judgment most excell
In Angling *or its* praise: *where commendation*
First charms, then makes an art a recreation.
　　'Twas *so to me: who* saw *the cheerful* Spring
Pictur'd in every meadow, *heard* birds *sing*
Sonnets *in every* grove, *saw* fishes *play*
In *the cool* crystal streams, *like* lambs *in* May:
And they may play, till Anglers *read this* book;
But after, 'tis a wise fish *scrapes a* hook.

Jo. FLOUD, Mr. of Arts

To *the Reader of the* Compleat Angler.

First mark the Title well; my Friend that gave it

Has made it good; this book deserves to have it.
For *he that views it with judicious looks,*
Shall find it full of art, baits, lines, *and* hooks.
   The world *the* river *is; both you and* I,
And all mankind, are either fish *or* fry:
If *we pretend to reason, first or last*
His *baits will tempt us, and his hooks hold fast.*
Pleasure *or profit, either prose or rhime,*
If *not at first will doubtless take 's in time.*
   Here *sits in secret blest* Theology,
Waited *upon by grave* Philosophy,
Both natural *and* moral; History
Deck'd *and adorn'd with flowers of* Poetry;
The *matter and expression striving which*
Shall *most excell in worth, yet not seem rich:*
There *is no danger in his* baits; *that* hook
Will *prove the safest, that is surest took.*
   Nor *are we caught alone, but (which is best)*
We *shall be wholsom, and be toothsom drest:*
Drest *to be fed, not to be fed upon;*
And *danger of a surfeit here is none.*
The *solid food of serious* Contemplation
Is *sauc'd here, with such harmless recreation,*
That *an* ingenuous *and* religious *mind*
Cannot *inquire for more than it may find*
Ready *at once prepar'd, either t' excite*
Or *satisfie a curious appetite.*
   More *praise is due; for 'tis both positive*
And *truth, which once was interrogative,*

And *utter'd by the Poet then in jest,*
    Et piscatorem piscis amare potest.

C. H., *Mr. of Arts.*

To my dear Friend, Mr. Iz. *Walton,* in praise of
        Angling, which we both love.

Down by this smooth streams wandering side,
Adorn'd and perfum'd with the pride
Of Flora's Wardrobe, where the shrill
Aerial Quire express their skill,
First in alternate melody,
And then in chorus all agree.
Whilst the charm'd fish, as ecstasi'd
With sounds, to his own throat deny'd,
Scorns his dull Element, and springs
I' th' air, as if his Fins were wings.
    'Tis here that pleasures sweet and high
Prostrate to our embraces lye.
Such as to Body, Soul, or Fame
Create no sickness, sin or shame.
Roses not fenc'd with pricks grow here,
No sting to th' Honey-bag is near.
But (what's perhaps their prejudice)
They difficulty want and price.
    An obvious Rod, a twist of hair,
With hook hid in an insect, are
Engines of sport, would fit the wish
O' th' Epicure and fill his dish.
    In this clear stream let fall a Grub,

And *straight take up a* Dace *or* Chub.
I' *th' mud, your worm provokes a* Snig,
Which being fast, if it prove big,
The Gotham *folly will be found*
Discreet, e're ta'ne she must be drown'd.
The Tench (*Physician of the* Brook)
In yon dead hole expects your hook,
Which having first your pastime been,
Serves then for meat or medicine.
Ambush'd behind that root doth stay
A Pike, *to catch and be a prey.*
The treacherous Quill *in this slow stream*
Betrayes the hunger of a Bream.
And at that nimbler Ford (*no doubt*)
Your false flye cheats a speckled Trout.
   When you these creatures wisely chuse
To practise on, which to your use
Owe their creation, and when
Fish from your arts do rescue men,
To plot, delude, and circumvent,
Ensnare and spoil, is innocent.
Here by these crystal streams you may
Preserve a Conscience *clear as they,*
And when by sullen thoughts you find
Your harassed, not busied, mind
In sable melancholly clad,
Distemper'd, serious, turning sad;
Hence fetch your cure, cast in your bait,
All anxious thoughts and cares will straight

Fly *with such speed, they'l seem to be*
Possest with the Hydrophobie.
The waters calmness in your breast,
And smoothness on your brow shall rest.
  Away with sports of charge and noise,
Sweeter are cheap and silent toyes.
Such as Actaeons *game pursue,*
Their fate oft makes the Tale *seem true.*
The sick or sullen Hawk *to day*
Flyes not; to-morrow, quite away.
Patience and Purse to Cards and Dice
Too oft are made a sacrifice:
The Daughters dowre, th' inheritance
O' th' son, depend on one mad chance.
The harms and mischiefs, which th' abuse
Of wine doth every day produce,
Make good the doctrine of the Turks,
That in each grape a devil lurks.
And by yon fading sapless tree,
'Bout which the Ivye *twin'd you see,*
His fate's foretold, who fondly places
His bliss in womans soft embraces.
All pleasures, but the Anglers, bring
I' th' tail repentance like a sting.
  Then on these banks let me sit down,
Free from the toilsom Sword and Gown,
And pity those that do affect
To conquer Nations and protect.
My Reed affords such true content,

Delights so sweet and innocent,
As seldom fall unto the lot
Of Sceptres, though they'r justly got.

THO. WEAVER, *Mr. of Arts.*

To the Readers of my most ingenious Friends Book,
The Compleat Angler.

HE *that both knew and writ the lives of men,*
   Such as were once, but must not be agen:
   Witness his matchless Donne *and* Wootten, *by*
   Whose aid he could their speculations try:
He *that convers'd with* Angels, *such as were*
   Ouldsworth *and* Featly, *each a shining star*
   Shewing the way to Bethlem; *each a Saint;*
   Compar'd to whom our Zelots *now but paint:*
He *that our pious and learn'd* Morley *knew,*
   And from him suck'd wit *and* devotion *too:*
He *that from these such excellencies fetch'd,*
   That He could tell how high and far they reach'd;
   What learning this, what graces th' other had;
   And in what sev'ral dress each soul was clad.

Reader, *this* HE, *this* Fisherman *comes forth,*
And in these Fishers weeds would shroud his worth.
Now his mute Harp is on a Willow hung,
With which when finely toucht, and fitly strung,
He could friends passions for these times allay;
Or chain his fellow-Anglers from their prey.
But now the musick of his pen is still,

And he sits by a brook watching a quill:
Where with a fixt eye, and a ready hand,
He studies first to hook, and then to land
Some Trout, *or* Pearch, *or* Pike; *and having done,*
Sits on a bank, and tells how this was won,
And that escap'd his hook; which with a wile
Did eat the bit, and Fisherman beguile.
Thus whilst some vex they from their lands are
   thrown,
He joyes to think the waters are his own;
  And like the Dutch, *he gladly can agree*
  To live *at peace now, and have* fishing *free.*

    April 3. 1650.   Edw. Powel, *Mr. of Arts.*

    To my dear Brother, Mr. Iz. Walton, on his
        Compleat Angler.

This Book is so like you, and you like it,
For harmless Mirth, Expression, Art and Wit,
That I protest ingenuously 'tis true,
I love this Mirth, Art, Wit, the Book, and You.
                Rob. Floud, C.

Charissimo amicissimoque Fratri Domino Isaaco Wal-
    ton, *Artis Piscatoriae peritissimo.*

Unicus est Medicus reliquorum piscis, et istis
  Fas quibus est Medicum tangere, certa salus.
Hic typus est Salvatoris mirandus Jesu,

[1]*Litera mysterium quaelibet hujus habet.*
Hunc cupio, hunc capias (bone frater Arundinis)
    ἰχθύν;
[2]*Solveret hic pro me debita, teque Deo.*
Piscis is est, et piscator, (mihi credito) qualem
    Vel piscatorem piscis amare velit.

HENRY BAGLEY, Artium Magister.

---

[1] Ἰχθὺς   *Piscis.*   θ Θεοῦ   *Dei.*
  I Ἰησοῦς   *Jesus.*   υ Υἱὸς   *Filius.*
  χ Χριστὸς   *Christus.*   ς Σωτὴρ   *Salvator.*
[2] Matt. 17, 27, the last words of the chapter.

THE
COMPLEAT ANGLER

OR THE CONTEMPLATIVE MANS RECREATION

CHAPTER I: A *Conference betwixt an* Angler, *a* Faulkner, *and a* Hunter, *each commending his Recreation.*

PISCATOR

VENATOR   AUCEPS

PISC. You are well overtaken, Gentlemen, a good morning to you both; I have stretched my legs up *Tottenham-hill* to overtake you, hoping your business may occasion you towards *Ware* this fine fresh *May* morning.

VENA. Sir, I for my part shall almost answer your hopes, for my purpose is to drink my morning draught at the *Thatcht House* in *Hodsden,* and I think not to rest till I come thither, where I have appointed a friend or two to meet me: but for this Gentleman that you see with me, I know not how far he intends his journey; he came so lately into my company, that I have scarce had time to ask him the question.

AUC. Sir, I shall by your favour bear you company as far as *Theobalds,* and there leave you, for then I turn up to a friends house who mews a Hawk for me, which I now long to see.

VENA. Sir, we are all so happy as to have a fine, fresh, cool morning, and I hope we shall each be the happier in the others company. And Gentlemen, that I may not lose yours, I shall either abate or amend my pace to enjoy it; knowing that (as the Italians say) *Good company in a journey makes the way to seem the shorter.*

AUC. It may do so Sir, with the help of good discourse, which methinks we may promise from you that both look and speak so cheerfully: and for my part I promise you, as an invitation to it, that I will be as free and open hearted, as discretion will allow me to be with strangers.

VENA. And Sir, I promise the like.

PISC. I am right glad to hear your answers, and in confidence you speak the truth, I shall put on a boldnesse to ask you Sir, Whether businesse or pleasure caused you to be so early up, and walk so fast, for this other Gentleman hath declared he is going to see a Hawk, that a friend mews for him.

VENA. Sir mine is a mixture of both, a little businesse and more pleasure, for I intend this day to do all my businesse, and then bestow another day or two in hunting the *Otter,* which a friend that I go to meet, tells me, is much pleasanter than any other chase whatsoever; howsoever I mean to try it; for to-morrow morning we shall meet a pack of Otter dogs of *noble*

Mr. *Sadlers* upon *Amwell* *Hill,* who will be there so early, that they intend to prevent the Sun-rising.

PISC. Sir, my fortune has answered my desires, and my purpose is to bestow a day or two in helping to destroy some of those villanous vermin, for I hate them perfectly, because they love fish so well, or rather, because they destroy so much; indeed so much, that in my judgment all men that keep *Otter-dogs* ought to have pensions from the King to incourage them to destroy the very breed of those base *Otters,* they do so much mischief.

VENA. But what say you to the Foxes of the Nation, would not you as willingly have them destroyed? for doubtless they do as much mischief as *Otters* do.

PISC. Oh Sir if they do, it is not so much to me and my fraternity as those base Vermine the *Otters* do.

AUC. Why Sir, I pray, of what Fraternity are you, that you are so angry with the poor *Otters?*

PISC. I am (Sir) a brother of the *Angle,* and therefore an enemy to the *Otter*: for you are to note, that we Anglers all love one another, and therefore do I hate the *Otter* both for my own and for their sakes who are of my brotherhood.

VENA. And I am a lover of Hounds, I have followed many a pack of dogs many a mile, and heard many merry men make sport and scoff at Anglers.

AUC. And I profess myself a Faulkner, and have heard many grave serious men pity them, 'tis such a heavy, contemptible, dull recreation.

PISC. You know Gentlemen, 'tis an easie thing to scoff at any Art or Recreation; a little *wit* mixt with ill nature, confidence, and *malice,* will do it; but though they often venture boldly, yet they are often caught even in their own trap, according to that of *Lucian,* the father of the family of Scoffers.

> *Lucian* well skill'd in scoffing, this hath writ,
> Friend, that's your folly which you think your wit:
> This you vent oft, void both of wit and fear,
> Meaning another, when your self you jeere.

If to this you add what *Solomon* sayes of Scoffers, That *they are abomination to mankind.* Let him that thinks fit be a Scoffer still, but I account them enemies to me, and to all that love *vertue* and *Angling.*

And for you that have heard many grave serious men pity Anglers; let me tell you Sir, there be many men that are by others taken to be serious grave men, which we contemn and pity. Men that are taken to be grave, because Nature hath made them of a sowre complexion, money-getting-men, men that spend all their time first in getting, and next in anxious care to keep it; men that are condemned to be rich, and then always busie or discontented: for these poor-rich-men, we Anglers pity them perfectly, and stand in no need to borrow their thoughts to think our selves happy. No, no, Sir, we enjoy a contentednesse above the reach of such dispositions, and as the learned and ingenuous *Mountagne*[1] sayes like himself freely, 'When my Cat

[1] In Apol. for Ra. Sebond.

and I entertain each other with mutual apish tricks (as playing with a garter) who knowes but that I make my Cat more sport than she makes me? shall I conclude her to be simple, that has her time to begin or refuse sportiveness as freely as I my self have? Nay, who knowes but that it is a defect of my not understanding her language (for doubtless Cats talk and reason with one another) that we agree no better: and who knows but that she pitties me for being no wiser, and laughs and censures my follie for making sport for her when we play together.'

Thus freely speaks *Mountagne* concerning Cats, and I hope I may take as great a liberty to blame any man, and laugh at him too, let him be never so serious, that hath not heard what Anglers can say in the justification of their Art and Recreation, which I may again tell you is so full of pleasure, that we need not borrow their thoughts to think our selves happy.

VENA. Sir, you have almost amazed me, for though I am no scoffer, yet I have (I pray let me speak it without offence) alwayes looked upon Anglers as more patient and more simple men, then I fear I shall find you to be.

PISC. Sir, I hope you will not judge my earnestness to be impatience: and for my *simplicity,* if by that you mean a harmlessness, or that simplicity which was usually found in the primitive Christians, who were (as most Anglers are) quiet men, and followers of peace; men that were so simply-wise, as not to sell their Consciences to buy riches, and with them vexation and a fear to die. If you mean such simple men as lived in those times when there were fewer Lawyers; when men might have had a Lordship safely conveyed to them in a piece of Parchment no bigger than your hand (though several sheets will not do it safely in this wiser age) I say, Sir, if you take us Anglers to be such simple men as I have spoke of, then my self and those of my Profession will be glad to be so understood: But if by simplicity you meant to express a general defect in those that profess and practise the excellent art of Angling, I hope in time to disabuse you, and make the contrary appear so evidently, that if you will but have patience to hear me, I shall remove all the Anticipations that discourse, or time, or prejudice have possess'd you with against that laudable and ancient art; for I know it is worthy the *knowledge* and *practice* of a wise man.

But (Gentlemen) though I be able to do this, I am not so unmannerly as to engross all the discourse to my self; and, therefore you two having declared your selves, the one to be a lover of *Hawks,* the other of *Hounds,* I shall be most glad to hear what you can say in the commendation of that Recreation which you love and practise; and having heard what you can say, I shall be glad to exercise your attention with what I can say concerning my own Recreation, and by this means we shall make the way to seem the shorter: and if you like my motion, I would have Mr. *Faulkner* to begin.

AUC. Your motion is consented to with all my heart, and to testifie it I will begin as you have desired me.

And first, for the Element that I use to trade in, which is the Air, an Element of more worth than weight, an Element that doubtless exceeds both the Earth and Water; for though I sometimes deal in both, yet the Air is most properly mine, I and my Hawks use that most, and it yields us most recreation; it stops not the high soaring of my noble generous *Falcon*; in it she ascends to such an height, as the dull eyes of beasts and fish are not able to reach to; their bodies are too gross for such high elevations: in the Air my troops of Hawks soar up on high, and when they are lost in the sight of men, then they attend upon and converse with the gods; therefore I think my *Eagle* is so justly styled, *Joves faithful servant in Ordinary*: and that very *Falcon,* that I am now going to see, deserves no meaner a title, for she usually in her flight endangers her self, (like the son of *Dedalus*) to have her wings scorch'd by the Suns heat, but her mettle makes her careless of danger, for she then heeds nothing, but makes her nimble Pinions cut the fluid air, and so makes her high way over the steepest mountains and deepest rivers, and in her glorious carere looks with contempt upon those high Steeples and magnificent Palaces which we adore and wonder at; from which height I can make her to descend by a word from my mouth (which she both knows and obeyes) to accept of meat from my hand, to own me for her master, to go home with me, and be willing the next day to afford me the like recreation.

And more, this Element of Air which I profess to trade in, the worth of it is such, and it is of such necessity, that no creature whatsoever, not onely those numerous creatures that feed on the face of the earth, but those various creatures that have their dwelling within the waters, every creature that hath life in its Nostrils stands in need of my Element. The waters cannot preserve the fish without Air, witness the not-breaking of Ice in an extream Frost; the reason is, for that if the inspiring and expiring Organ of any animal be stopt, it suddenly yields to Nature, and dies. Thus necessary is Air to the existence both of fish and beasts, nay, even to man himself; that Air or breath of life, with which God at first inspired Mankind, he, if he wants it, dies presently, becomes a sad object to all that loved and beheld him, and in an instant turns to putrefaction.

Nay more, the very birds of the air (those that be not Hawks) are both so many and so useful and pleasant to mankind, that I must not let them pass without some observations: They both feed and refresh him; feed him with their choice bodies, and refresh him with their heavenly voices. I will not undertake to mention the several kinds of Fowl by which this is done; and his curious palate pleased by day, and which with their very excrements afford him a soft lodging at night. These I will pass by, but not those little nimble Musicians of the air, that warble forth their curious

Ditties, with which Nature hath furnished them to the shame of Art.

As first the *Lark,* when she means to rejoyce, to chear her self and those that hear her, she then quits the earth, and sings as she ascends higher into the air, and having ended her heavenly imployment, grows then mute and sad to think she must descend to the dull earth, which she would not touch but for necessity.

How do the *Black-bird* and *Thrassel* with their melodious voices bid welcome to the cheerful Spring, and in their fixed Moneths warble forth such ditties as no art or instrument can reach to?

Nay, the smaller birds also do the like in their particular seasons, as namely the *Leverock,* the *Tit-lark,* the little *Linnet,* and the honest *Robin,* that loves mankind both alive and dead.

But the *Nightingale* (another of my Airy Creatures) breathes such sweet lowd musick out of her little instrumental throat, that it might make mankind to think Miracles are not ceased. He that at midnight (when the very labourer sleeps securely) should hear (as I have very often) the clear aires, the sweet descants, the natural rising and falling, the doubling and redoubling of her voice, might well be lifted above earth, and say, Lord, what Musick hast thou provided for the Saints in Heaven, when thou affordest bad men such musick on earth!

And this makes me the lesse to wonder at the many *Aviaries* in *Italy,* or at the great charge of *Varro* his

A*viarie,* the ruines of which are yet to be seen in *Rome,* and is still so famous there, that it is reckoned for one of those Notables which men of forraign Nations either record or lay up in their memories when they return from travel.

This for the birds of pleasure, of which very much more might be said. My next shall be of Birds of Political use; I think 'tis not to be doubted that Swallowes have been taught to carry Letters betwixt two Armies. But 'tis certain that when the Turks besieged *Malta* or *Rodes* (I now remember not which 'twas) *Pigeons* are then related to carry and recarry Letters. And Mr. G. *Sandis* in his Travells (*fol.* 269) relates it to be done betwixt *Aleppo* and *Babylon.* But if that be disbelieved, 'tis not to be doubted that the *Dove* was sent by N*oah,* to give him notice of Land, when to him all appeared to be Sea, and the Dove proved a faithful messenger. And for the Sacrifices of the Law, a pair of *Turtle Doves* or young *Pigeons* were as well accepted as costly *Bulls* and *Rams.* And when God would feed the Prophet E*lijah* (1 K*ing.* 17), after a kind of miraculous manner, he did it by *Ravens,* who brought him meat morning and evening. Lastly, the Holy Ghost when he descended visibly upon our Saviour, did it by assuming the shape of a *Dove.* And to conclude this part of my Discourse, pray remember these wonders were done by birds of the Air, the Element in which they and I take so much pleasure.

There is also a little contemptible winged Creature

(an inhabitant of my Aerial Element) namely the laborous *Bee,* of whose *Prudence, Policy* and regular Government of their own Commonwealth I might say much, as also of their several kinds, and how useful their honey and wax is both for meat and Medicines to mankind; but I will leave them to their sweet labour, without the least disturbance, believing them to be all very busie amongst the herbs and flowers that we see nature puts forth this *May* morning.

And now to return to my Hawks from whom I have made too long a Digression; you are to note, that they are usually distinguished into two kinds; namely the long-winged and the short-winged Hawk: of the first kind, there be chiefly in use amongst us in this Nation,

The *Gerfalcon* and *Jerkin.*
The *Falcon* and *Tassel-gentel.*
The *Laner* and *Laneret.*
The *Bockerel* and *Bockeret.*
The *Saker* and *Sacaret.*
The *Marlin* and *Jack Marlin.*
The *Hoby* and *Jack.*
There is the *Stelletto* of *Spain.*
The *Bloud red Rook* from Turky.
The *Waskite* from *Virginia.*
And there is of short-winged Hawks
The *Eagle* and *Iron.*
The *Goshawk* and *Tarcel.*
The *Sparhawk* and *Musket.*
The French *Pye* of two sorts.

These are reckoned Hawks of note and worth, but we have also of an inferiour rank,

The *Stanyel,* the *Ringtail.*
The *Raven,* the *Buzzard.*
The forked *Kite,* the bald *Buzzard.*
The *Hen-driver,* and others that I forbear to name.

Gentlemen, if I should inlarge my Discourse to the observation of the *Eires,* the *Brancher,* the *Ramish Hawk,* the *Haggard,* and the two sorts of *Lentners,* and then treat of their several *Ayries,* their *Mewings,* rare order of casting, and the renovation of their *Feathers,* their reclaiming, dyeting, and then come to their rare stories of practice; I say, if I should enter into these, and many other observations that I could make, it would be much, very much pleasure to me: but least I should break the rules of Civility with you, by taking up more than the proportion of time allotted to me, I will here break off, and intreat you, Mr. *Venator,* to say what you are able in the commendation of Hunting, to which you are so much affected, and if time will serve, I will beg your favour for a further enlargement of some of those several heads of which I have spoken. But no more at present.

VENA. Well Sir, and I will now take my turn, and will first begin with a commendation of the earth, as you have done most excellently of the Air, the Earth being that Element upon which I drive my pleasant wholesome hungry trade. The Earth is a solid, settled Element; an Element most universally beneficiall both to man and beast; to men who have their several Recreations upon it, as Horse-races, Hunting, sweet smells, pleasant walks. The earth feeds man, and all those several beasts that both feed him, and afford him recreation: What pleasure doth man take in hunting the stately *Stag,* the generous *Buck,* the *Wild Boar,* the cunning *Otter,* the crafty *Fox,* and the fearful *Hare?* And if I may descend to a lower Game, what pleasure is it sometimes with Gins to betray the very vermine of the earth? as namely the *Fichat,* the *Fulimart,* the *Feret,* the *Pole-cat,* the *Mouldwarp,* and the like creatures that live upon the face, and within the bowels of the earth. How doth the earth bring forth *herbs, flowers* and *fruits,* both for *physick* and the *pleasure* of mankind? and above all, to me at least, the fruitful *Vine,* of which when I drink moderately, it clears my brain, chears my heart, and sharpens my wit. How could *Cleopatra* have feasted *Mark Antony* with eight Wild Boars roasted whole at one Supper, and other meat suitable, if the earth had not been a bountiful mother? But to pass by the mighty *Elephant,* which the earth breeds and nourisheth, and descend to the least of creatures, how doth the earth afford us a doctrinal example in the little *Pismire,* who in the Summer provides and layes up her Winter-provision, and teaches man to do the like? The earth feeds and carries those horses that carry us. If I would be prodigal of my time and your patience, what might not I say in commendations of the earth? That puts limits to the proud and raging *Sea,* and by that means preserves both man and beast, that it destroyes them not; as we see it daily doth those that venture upon the sea, and are there ship wreckt, drowned, and left to feed Haddocks; when we that are so wise as to keep ourselves on *earth, walk,* and *talk,* and *live,* and *eat,* and *drink,* and go a *hunting:* of which recreation I will say a little, and then leave Mr. *Piscator* to the commendation of Angling.

Hunting is a game for Princes and noble persons; it hath been highly prized in all Ages; it was one of the qualifications that *Zenophon* bestowed on his *Cyrus,* that he was a Hunter of wild beasts. Hunting trains up the younger Nobility to the use of manly exercises in their riper age. What more manly exercise than *hunting the* Wild Bore, *the* Stag, *the* Buck, *the* Fox, or the Hare? How doth it preserve health, and increase strength and activity?

And for the Dogs that we use, who can commend their excellency to that height which they deserve? How perfect is the Hound at *smelling,* who never leaves or forsakes his sent, but follows it thorow so many changes and varieties of other sents, even over and in the water, and into the earth? What musique doth a pack of Dogs then make to any man, whose heart and ears are so happy as to be set to the tune of such instruments? How will a right *Greyhound* fix his eye on the best *Buck* in a *heard,* single him out and follow him, and him onely through a whole herd of Rascal game, and still know and kill him? For my

Hounds I know the language of them, and they know the language and meaning of one another as perfectly as we know the voices of those with whom we discourse daily.

I might enlarge myself in the commendation of *Hunting,* and of the noble Hound especially, as also of the docibleness of *dogs* in general; and I might make many observations of Land-creatures, that for composition, order, figure and constitution, approach nearest to the compleatness and understanding of man; especially of those creatures which M*oses* in the Law permitted to the Jews (which have cloven Hoofs, and chew the Cud), which I shall forbear to name, because I will not be so uncivil to Mr. P*iscator,* as not to allow him a time for the commendation of A*ngling,* which he calls an Art, but doubtless 'tis an easie one: and Mr. A*uceps,* I doubt we shall hear a watry discourse of it; but I hope 'twill not be a long one.

AUC. And I hope so too, though I fear it will.

PISC. Gentlemen, let not prejudice prepossesse you. I confesse my discourse is like to prove suitable to my Recreation, *calm* and *quiet*; we seldome take the name of God into our mouths, but it is either to praise him or pray to him; if others use it vainly in the midst of their recreations, so vainly as if they meant to conjure, I must tell you it is neither our fault nor our custom; we, we protest against it. But, pray remember I accuse no body; for as I would not make a *watry* discourse, so I would not put too much *vinegar* into it, nor would I raise the reputation of my own Art by the diminution or ruine of anothers. And so much for the Prologue to what I mean to say.

And now for the W*ater,* the Element that I trade in. The *water* is the eldest daughter of the Creation, the Element upon which the Spirit of God did first move, the Element which God commanded to bring forth living creatures abundantly; and without which those that inhabit the Land, even all creatures that have breath in their nostrils must suddenly return to putrefaction. M*oses* the great Law-giver and chief Philosopher, skilled in all the learning of the Egyptians, who was called the friend of God, and knew the mind of the Almighty, names this element the first in the Creation; this is the element upon which the Spirit of God did first move, and is the chief Ingredient in the Creation: Many Philosophers have made it to comprehend all the other Elements, but most allow it the chiefest in the mixtion of all living creatures.

There be that profess to believe that all bodies are made of *water,* and may be reduced back again to water onely: they endeavour to demonstrate it thus:

Take a W*illow* (or any like speedy growing plant) newly rooted in a box or barrel full of earth, weigh them all together exactly when the tree begins to grow, and then weigh all together after the tree is increased from its first rooting to weigh an hundred pound weight more than when it was first rooted and weighed; and you shall find this augment of the tree to be without the diminution of one dram of the earth.

Hence they infer this increase of wood to be from water of rain, or from dew, and not to be from any other Element. And they affirm, they can reduce this wood back again to water; and they affirm also the same may be done in any *animal* or *vegetable*. And this I take to be a fair testimony of the excellency of my element of water.

The W*ater* is more productive than the E*arth*. Nay, the earth hath no fruitfulness without showers or dews; all the *herbs,* and *flowers,* and *fruit* are produced and thrive by the water; and the very Minerals are fed by streams that run under ground, whose natural course carries them to the tops of many high mountains, as we see by several springs breaking forth on the tops of the highest hills, and this is also witnessed by the daily tryal and testimony of several Miners.

Nay, the increase of those creatures that are bred and fed in the water, are not onely more and more miraculous, but more advantagious to man, not onely for the lengthning of his life, but for the preventing of sicknesse; for 'tis observed by the most learned Physicians, that the casting off of Lent and other Fish-dayes (which hath not onely given the Lie to so many learned, pious, wise Founders of Colledges, for which we should be ashamed) hath doubtless been the chief cause of those many putride, shaking, intermitting Agues, unto which this Nation of ours is now more subject than those wiser Countries that feed on Herbs, Sallets, and plenty of Fish; of which it is observed in Story, that the greatest part of the world now do. And it may be fit to remember that *Moses* (*Lev.* 11. 9. *Deut.* 14. 9.) appointed Fish to be the chief diet for the best Common-wealth that ever yet was.

And it is observable not onely that there are *Fish*, (as namely the *Whale*) three times as big as the mighty Elephant, that is so fierce in battel; but that the mightiest Feasts have been of Fish. The *Romans* in the height of their glory have made Fish the mistress of all their entertainments; they have had Musick to usher in their *Sturgeons*, *Lampreyes*, and *Mullet*, which they would purchase at rates rather to be wondred at than believed. He that shall view the Writings of *Macrobius* or *Varro*, may be confirmed and informed of this, and of the incredible value of their Fish, and Fish-ponds.

But, Gentlemen, I have almost lost my self, which I confess I may easily do in this Philosophical Discourse; I met with most of it very lately (and I hope happily) in a conference with a most learned Physician, a dear Friend, that loves both me and my Art of Angling. But however I will wade no deeper in these mysterious Arguments, but pass to such Observations as I can manage with more pleasure, and less fear of running into error. But I must not yet forsake the Waters, by whose help we have so many known advantages.

And first (to passe by the miraculous cures of our known *Baths*) how advantagious is the *Sea* for our daily *Traffique*, without which we could not now subsist? How does it not onely furnish us with food and physick for the bodies, but with such observations for the mind as ingenious persons would not want?

How ignorant had we been of the beauty of *Florence*, of the *Monuments, Urns,* and *Rarities* that yet remain in, and near unto old and new *Rome* (so many as it is said will take up a years time to view, and afford to each but a convenient consideration); and therefore it is not to be wondred at, that so learned and devout a Father as St. *Jerome*, after his wish to have seen Christ in the flesh, and to have heard St. *Paul* preach, makes his third wish to have seen *Rome* in her glory; and that beauty is not yet all lost, for what pleasure is it to see the Monuments of *Livy*, the choicest of the Historians; of *Tully*, the best of Orators; and to see the Bay-trees that now grow out of the very Tomb of *Virgil*? These to any that love Learning. But what pleasure is it to a devout Christian to see there the humble house in which Saint *Paul* was content to dwell; and to view the many rich *Statues* that are there made in honour of his memory? nay, to see the very place in which Saint *Peter* and he lie buried together? These are in and near to *Rome*. And how much more doth it please the pious curiosity of a Christian to see that place, on which the blessed Saviour of the world was pleased to humble himself, and to take our nature upon him, and to converse with men; to see Mount *Sion, Jerusalem,* and the very Sepulchre of our Jesus? How may it beget and heighten the zeal of a Christian to see the Devotions that are daily paid to him at that place? Gentlemen, lest I forget my self I will stop here, and remember you, that but for my Element of water the Inhabitants of this poor Island must remain ignorant that such things have yet a being.

Gentlemen, I might both enlarge and lose myself in such like Arguments; I might tell you that Almighty God is said to have spoken to a *Fish,* but never to a *Beast*; that he hath made a W*hale* a Ship to carry and set his prophet J*onah* safe on the appointed shore. Of these I might speake, but I must in manners break off, for I see T*heobalds* house. I cry you mercy for being so long, and thank you for your patience.

AUC. Sir, my pardon is easily granted you: I except against nothing that you have said, neverthelesse I must part with you at this Park-wall, for which I am very sorry; but I assure you Mr. P*iscator,* I now part with you full of good thoughts, not onely of your self, but your Recreation. And so Gentlemen, God keep you both.

PISC. Well, now Mr. V*enator* you shall neither want time nor my attention to hear you enlarge your Discourse concerning Hunting.

VENA. Not I Sir, I remember you said that A*ngling* it self was of great Antiquity, and a perfect Art, and an Art not easily attained to; and you have so won upon me in your former discourse, that I am very desirous to hear what you can say further concerning those particulars.

PISC. Sir, I did say so, and I doubt not but if you and I did converse together but a few hours, to leave you possest with the same high and happy thoughts that now possess me of it; not onely of the Antiquity of *Angling,* but that it deserves commendations, and that it is an Art, and an Art worthy the knowledge and practise of a wise man.

VENA. Pray Sir speak of them what you think fit; for we have yet five miles to the *Thatcht*-House, during which walk I dare promise you my patience and diligent attention shall not be wanting. And if you shall make that to appear which you have undertaken, first, that it is an Art, and an Art worth the learning, I shall beg that I may attend you a day or two a fishing, and that I may become your Scholar, and be instructed in the Art it self which you so much magnifie.

PISC. O Sir, doubt not but that *Angling* is an Art, and an Art worth your learning: the Question is rather whether you be capable of learning it? for *Angling* is somewhat like *Poetry,* men are to be born so: I mean, with inclinations to it, though both may be heightned by practice and experience: but he that hopes to be a good *Angler* must not onely bring an inquiring, searching, observing wit, but he must bring a large measure of hope and patience, and a love and propensity to the Art it self; but having once got and practis'd it, then doubt not but *Angling* will prove to be so pleasant, that it will prove like Vertue, a reward to it self.

VENA. Sir, I am now become so full of expectation that I long much to have you proceed, and in the order that you propose.

PISC. Then first, for the *antiquity* of *Angling,* of which I shall not say much, but onely this; Some say it is as ancient as *Deucalions* Flood: others, that *Belus,* who was the first Inventor of Godly and vertuous Recreations, was the first Inventor of *Angling*: and some others say (for former times have had their disquisitions about the Antiquity of it) that *Seth,* one of the sons of *Adam,* taught it to his Sons, and that by them it was derived to posterity: others say, that he left it ingraven on those pillars which he erected, and trusted to preserve the knowledge of the *Mathematicks, Musick,* and the rest of that precious knowledge, and those useful Arts which by Gods appointment or allowance and his noble industry were thereby preserved from perishing in *Noahs* flood.

These, Sir, have been the opinions of several men, that have possibly endeavoured to make *Angling* more ancient than is needful, or may well be warranted; but for my part, I shall content my self in telling you that Angling is much more ancient than the Incarnation of our Saviour; for in the Prophet *Amos* mention is made of *fish-hooks*; and in the Book of *Job* (which was long before the days of *Amos,* for that book is said to be writ by *Moses*) mention is made also of Fish-hooks, which must imply Anglers in those times.

But my worthy friend, as I would rather prove my self a *Gentleman* by being *learned,* and *humble, valiant,* and *inoffensive, vertuous,* and *communicable,* than by any fond ostentation of riches, or wanting these vertues my self, boast that these were in my Ancestors (and yet I grant that where a noble and ancient descent and such merits meet in any man, it is a double dignification of that person:) So if this Antiquity of *Angling* (which for my part I have not forced) shall like an ancient family, be either an honour or an ornament to this vertuous Art which I profess to love and practice, I shall be the gladder that I made an accidental mention of the antiquity of it; of which I shall say no more but proceed to that just commendation which I think it deserves.

And for that I shall tell you, that in ancient times a debate hath risen (and it remains yet unresolved) Whether the happiness of man in this world doth consist more in *Contemplation* or *action*.

Concerning which some have endeavoured to maintain their opinion of the first, by saying, *That the nearer we Mortals come to God by way of imitation, the more happy we are.* And they say, *That God enjoys himself onely by a contemplation of his own infinitenesse, Eternity, Power and Goodness,* and the like. And upon this ground many Cloysteral men of great learning and devotion prefer *Contemplation* before *Action*. And many of the Fathers seem to approve this opinion, as may appear in their Commentaries upon the words of our Saviour to *Martha, Luke* 10. 41, 42.

And on the contrary, there want not men of equal authority and credit, that prefer *action* to be the more excellent, as namely, *experiments in Physick, and the application of it, both for the ease and prolongation of mans life*; by which each man is enabled to act and do good to others; either to serve his Countrey, or do good to particular persons; and they say also, *That action is Doctrinal, and teaches both art and vertue, and is a maintainer of humane society*; and for these and other like reasons to be preferred before *contemplation*.

Concerning which two opinions I shall forbear to add a third, by declaring my own, and rest my self contented in telling you (my very worthy friend) that both these meet together, and do most properly belong to the most *honest, ingenuous, quiet*, and *harmlesse* art of *Angling*.

And first, I shall tell you what some have observed, (and I have found it to be a real truth) that the very sitting by the Rivers side is not onely the quietest and fittest place for *contemplation*, but will invite an Angler to it: and this seems to be maintained by the learned *Pet. du Moline*, who (in his Discourse of the Fulfilling of Prophecies) observes, that when God intended to reveal any future events or high notions to his Prophets, he then carried them either to the *Deserts* or the *Sea-shore*, that having so separated them from amidst the press of *people*, and *businesse*, and the cares of the world, he might settle their minds in a quiet repose, and there make them fit for Revelation.

And this seems also to be intimated by the Children of *Israel* (*Psal.* 137.) who having in a sad condition banished all mirth and musique from their pensive hearts, and having hung up their then mute Harps upon the Willow-trees growing by the Rivers of *Baby-*

lon, sate down upon those banks bemoaning the ruines of *Sion,* and contemplating their own sad condition.

And an ingenuous *Spaniard* sayes, *That Rivers and the Inhabitants of the watry Element were made for wise men to contemplate, and fools to passe by without consideration.* And though I will not rank myself in the number of the first, yet give me leave to free my self from the last, by offering to you a short contemplation, first of *Rivers,* and then of *Fish,* concerning which I doubt not but to give you many observations that will appear very considerable: I am sure they have appeared so to me, and made many an hour passe away more pleasantly, as I have sate quietly on a flowery Bank by a calm River, and contemplated what I shall now relate to you.

And first concerning Rivers, there be divers wonders reported of them by Authors of such credit, that we need not deny them an Historical Faith.

As namely of a River in *Epirus,* that puts out any lighted Torch, and kindles any Torch that was not lighted. Some Waters being drunk cause madnesse, some drunkennesse, and some laughter to death. The River *Selarus* in a few hours turns a rod or wand to be stone: and our *Cambden* mentions the like in *England,* and the like in *Lochmere* in *Ireland.* There is also a River in *Arabia,* of which all the sheep that drink thereof have their wool turned into a Vermillion colour. And one of no lesse credit than *Aristotle* tells us of a merry river (the river Elusina) that dances at the noise of musique, for with musique it bubbles, dances and grows sandy, and so continues till the musique ceases, but then it presently returns to its wonted calmness and clearness. And *Cambden* tells us of a Well near to *Kerby* in *Westmoreland,* that ebbs and flows several times every day: and he tells us of a river in *Surry* (it is called *Mole*), that after it has run several miles, being opposed by hills, finds or makes itself a way under ground, and breaks out again so far off, that the Inhabitants thereabout boast (as the *Spaniards* do of their River *Anus*) that they feed divers flocks of sheep upon a Bridge. And, lastly, for I would not tire your patience, one of no lesse authority than *Josephus* that learned Jew, tells us of a River in *Judea,* that runs swiftly all the six days of the week. and stands still and rests all their *Sabbath.*

But, Sir, lest this Discourse may seem tedious, I shall give it a sweet conclusion out of that holy Poet Mr. *George* H*erbert* his Divine Contemplation on Gods Providence:

Lord, who hath praise enough, nay, who hath any?
None can express thy works, but he that knows them,
And none can know thy works, they are so many,
And so compleat, but onely he that ows them.

We all acknowledge both thy power and love
To be exact, transcendent and divine;
Who dost so strangely and so sweetly move,
Whilst all things have their end, yet none but thine.

Wherefore, most sacred Spirit, I here present
For me, and all my fellows praise to thee;

And just it is that I should pay the rent,
Because the benefit accrues to me.

And as concerning fish, in that Psalm (P*sal.* 104) wherein for height of Poetry and Wonders the Prophet *David* seems even to exceed himself, how doth he there express himself in choice Metaphors, even to the amazement of a contemplative Reader, concerning the S*ea,* the R*ivers,* and the F*ish* therein contained? And the great Naturalist P*liny* sayes, *That Natures great and wonderful power is more demonstrated in the Sea than on the Land.* And this may appear by the numerous and various creatures, inhabiting both in and about that Element; as to the Readers of G*esner,* R*andeletius,* P*liny,* A*usonius,* A*ristotle,* and others, may be demonstrated. But I will sweeten this Discourse also out of a Contemplation in Divine D*ubartas,* who sayes,[1]

God quickned in the sea and in the rivers,
So many fishes of so many features,
That in the waters we may see all creatures,
Even all that on the earth is to be found,
As if the world were in deep waters drown'd.
For seas (as well as skies) have Sun, Moon, Stars;
(As well as air) Swallows, Rooks, and Stares;
(As well as earth) Vines, Roses, Nettles, Melons,
Mushrooms, Pinks, Gilliflowers, and many millions
Of other plants, more rare, more strange than these,
As very fishes living in the seas:
As also Rams, Calves, Horses, Hares, and Hogs,

[1] *Dubartas in the fifth day.*

Wolves, Urchins, Lions, Elephants, and Dogs;
Yea, Men and Maids, and which I most admire,
The mitred Bishop, and the cowled Fryer.
Of which, examples but a few years since,
Were shown the Norway *and* Polonian *prince.*

These seem to be wonders, but have had so many confirmations from men of learning and credit, that you need not doubt them; nor are the number, nor the various shapes of fishes, more strange or more fit for *contemplation,* than their different natures, inclinations and actions; concerning which I shall beg your patient ear a little longer.

The *Cuttle-fish* will cast a long gut out of her throat, which (like as an Angler doth his line) she sendeth forth and pulleth in again at her pleasure, according as she sees some little fish come near to her; and the *Cuttle-fish*[1] (being then hid in the gravel) lets the smaller fish nibble and bite the end of it, at which time she by little and little draws the smaller fish so near to her, that she may leap upon her, and then catches and devours her: and for this reason some have called this fish the *Sea-angler.*

And there is a fish called a **Hermit,** that at a certain age gets into a dead fishes shell, and like a Hermite dwells there alone, studying the wind and weather, and so turns her shell that she makes it defend her from the injuries that they would bring upon her.

There is also a fish called by *Elian* (in his 9. book

[1] *Mount. Essayes: and others affirm this.*

of Living Creatures, Chap. 16.) the *Adonis,* or Darling of the Sea; so called, because it is a loving and innocent fish, a fish that hurts nothing that hath life, and is at peace with all the numerous Inhabitants of that vast watery Element: and truly I think most Anglers are so disposed to most of mankind.

And there are also lustful and chast Fishes, of which I shall give you examples.

And first, what *Dubartas* says of a fish called the *Sargus*; which (because none can expresse it better than he does) I shall give you in his own words, supposing it shall not have the less credit for being Verse, for he hath gathered this, and other observations out of Authors that have been great and industrious searchers into the secrets of Nature.

> *The Adult'rous* Sargus *doth not only change*
> *Wifes every day in the deep streams, but (strange)*
> *As if the honey of Sea-love delight*
> *Could not suffice his ranging appetite,*
> *Goes courting she-Goats on the grassie shore,*
> *Horning their husbands that had horns before.*

And the same Author writes concerning the *Cantharus,* that which you shall also hear in his own words.

> *But contrary, the constant* Cantharus,
> *Is ever constant to his faithful Spouse,*
> *In nuptial duties spending his chaste life,*
> *Never loves any but his own dear wife.*

Sir, but a little longer, and I have done.

VENA. Sir, take what libertie you think fit, for your discourse seems to be Musique, and charms me into an attention.

PISC. Why then Sir, I will take a little liberty to tell, or rather to remember you what is said of *Turtle-Doves*: First, that they silently plight their troth and marry; and that then, the Survivor scornes (as the *Thracian women* are said to do) to out-live his or her mate; and this is taken for such a truth, and if the Survivor shall ever couple with another, then not only the living, but the dead (be it either the He or the she) is denyed the *name* and *honour* of a true *Turtle-dove*.

And to parallel this Land Rarity, and teach mankind moral faithfulness, and to condemn those that talk of Religion, and yet come short of the moral faith of fish and fowl; Men that violate the Law affirmed by Saint *Paul* (*Rom.* 2. 14, 15.) to be writ in their hearts, (and which he sayes, shall at the last day condemn and leave them without excuse), I pray hearken to what *Du-bartas*[1] sings, (for the hearing of such conjugal faithfulness, will be Musick to all chaste ears) and therefore I pray hearken to what *Dubartas* sings of the *Mullet*.

> *But for chaste love the* Mullet *hath no peer;*
> *For, if the Fisher hath surpriz'd her pheer,*
> *As mad with wo, to shore she followeth,*
> *Prest to consort him both in life and death.*

[1] *Dubartas fifth day.*

On the contrary, what shall I say of the *House-Cock,* which treads any Hen, and then (contrary to the *Swan,* the *Partridge* and *Pigeon*) takes no care to hatch, to feed or to cherish his own brood, but is senseless though they perish.

And 'tis considerable, that the *Hen* (which because she also takes any *Cock,* expects it not) who is sure the Chickens be her own, hath by a moral impression her care and affection to her own Brood more than doubled, even to such a height, that our Saviour in expressing his love to *Jerusalem* (*Mat.* 23. 37.) quotes her for an example of tender affection, as his Father had done *Job* for a patern of patience.

And to parallel this *Cock,* there be divers fishes that cast their Spawn on flags or stones, and then leave it uncovered, and exposed to become a prey, and be devoured by Vermine or other fishes: but other fishes (as namely the *Barbel*) take such care for the preservation of their seed, that (unlike to the *Cock* or the *Cuckoe*) they mutually labour (both the Spawner and the Melter) to cover their Spawn with sand, or watch it, or hide it in some secret place unfrequented by Vermine or by any Fish but themselves.

Sir, these Examples may, to you and others, seem strange; but they are testified some by *Aristotle,* some by *Pliny,* some by *Gesner,* and by many others of credit, and are believed and known by divers, both of wisdom and experience, to be a Truth; and indeed are (as I said at the beginning) fit for the contemplation of a most serious and a most pious man. And doubtless this made the Prophet *David* say, *They that occupy themselves in deep waters see the wonderful works of God*: indeed such wonders and pleasures too as the land affords not.

And that they be fit for the contemplation of the most prudent, and pious, and peaceable men, seems to be testifyed by the practice of so many devout and contemplative men, as the *Patriarchs* and *Prophets* of old, and of the *Apostles* of our Saviour in these later times; of which twelve he chose four that were Fishermen, whom he inspired and sent to publish his blessed Will to the *Gentiles, freedom from the incumbrances of the Law, and a new way to everlasting life*; this was the imployment of these Fishermen. Concerning which choice, some have made these Observations.

First, that he never reproved these for their Imployment or Calling, as he did the *Scribes* and the *Money-changers*. And secondly, he found that the hearts of such men by nature were fitted for contemplation and quietnesse; men of mild, and sweet, and peaceable spirits, as indeed most Anglers are: these men our blessed Saviour (who is observed to love to plant grace in good natures), though nothing be too hard for him, yet these men he chose to call from their irreprovable imployment of Fishing, and gave them grace to be his Disciples, and to follow him. I say four of twelve.

And it is observable, that it was our Saviours will, that these our four Fishermen should have a priority of nomination in the catalogue of his twelve Apostles,

(*Mat.* 10.) as namely first St. *Peter,* St. *Andrew,* St. *James* and St. *John,* and then the rest in their order.

And it is yet more observable, that when our blessed Saviour went up into the Mount, when he left the rest of his Disciples, and chose onely three to bear him company at his *Transfiguration,* that those three were all Fishermen. And it is to be believed, that all the other Apostles, after they betook themselves to follow Christ, betook themselves to be Fishermen too; for it is certain that the greater number of them were found together a Fishing by Jesus after his Resurrection, as is recorded in the 21. Chapter of St. *Johns* Gospel.

And since I have your promise to hear me with patience, I will take a liberty to look back upon an observation that hath been made by an ingenuous and learned man, who observes that God hath been pleased to allow those, whom he himself hath appointed to writ his holy Will in holy Writ, yet to express his Will in such Metaphors as their former affections or practice had inclined them to; and he brings *Solomon* for an example, who before his conversion was remarkably carnally-amorous; and after by Gods appointment writ that spiritual, holy, amorous Love-song (the *Canticles*) betwixt God and his Church, (in which he sayes she had E*yes like the fish-pools of Heshbon*).

And if this hold in reason as I see none to the contrary, then it may be probably concluded, that *Moses* (whom, I told you before, writ the Book of *Job*) and the Prophet *Amos,* who was a Shepherd, were both

Anglers, for you shall in all the Old Testament find Fish-hooks, I think but twice mentioned, namely, by meek *Moses* the friend of God, and by the humble Prophet *Amos*.

Concerning which last, namely the Prophet *Amos*, I shall make but this Observation, That he that shall read the *humble, lowly, plain style* of that *Prophet*, and compare it with the *high-glorious, eloquent style* of the Prophet *Isaiah* (though they be both equally true) may easily believe him to be, not only a Shepherd, but a good-natur'd, plain *Fisher-man*.

Which I do the rather believe, by comparing the affectionate, loving, lowly, humble Epistles of S. *Peter,* S. *James* and S. *John,* whom we know were all Fishers, with the glorious language and high Metaphors of S. *Paul,* who we may believe was not.

And for the lawfulness of Fishing: it may very well be maintained by our Saviours bidding St. *Peter* cast his hook into the water and catch a Fish, for money to pay Tribute to *Caesar*. And let me tell you, that angling is of high esteem, and of much use in other Nations. He that reads the Voyages of *Ferdinand Mendez Pinto,* shall find that there he declares to have found a King and several Priests a Fishing.

And he that reads *Plutarch* shall find that Angling was not contemptible in the dayes of *Mark Antony* and *Cleopatra,* and that they in the midst of their wonderful glory used Angling as a principal recreation. And let me tell you, that in the Scripture Angling is alwayes taken in the best sense; and that though hunting may be sometimes so taken, yet it is but seldom to be so understood. And let me adde this more, he that views the ancient Ecclesiastical Canons, shall find *Hunting* to be forbidden to Church-men, as being a toilsom, perplexing Recreation; and shall find *angling* allowed to *Clergy-men,* as being a harmlesse Recreation, a recreation that invites them to *contemplation* and *quietness.*

I might here enlarge myself, by telling you what commendations our learned *Perkins* bestowes on Angling: and how dear a lover, and great a practiser of it our learned Doctor *Whitaker* was, as indeed many others of great note have been. But I will content my self with two memorable men, that lived neer to our own time, whom I also take to have been ornaments to the Art of Angling.

The first is Doctor *Nowel* sometimes Dean of the Cathedral Church of Saint *Paul* in *London,* where his Monument stands yet undefaced; a man that in the Reformation of Queen *Elizabeth* (not that of *Henry the* VIII.) was so noted for his meek spirit, deep learning, prudence and piety, that the then Parliament and Convocation both, chose, injoyned and trusted him to be the man to make a Catechism for publick use, such a one as should stand as a rule for faith and manners to their posterity. And the good old man (though he was very learned, yet knowing that God leads us not to heaven by many nor by hard questions) like an honest Angler, made that *good, plain, unperplext* Catechism which is printed with our good old Service Book. I say, this good man was a dear lover, and constant prac-ticer of Angling, as any Age can produce; and his custome was to spend besides his fixt hours of prayer (those hours which by command of the Church were enjoyned the Clergy, and voluntarily dedicated to de-votion by many Primitive Christians): besides those hours, this good man was observed to spend a tenth part of his time in Angling; and also (for I have con-versed with those which have conversed with him) to bestow a tenth part of his Revenue, and usually all his fish, amongst the poor that inhabited near to those Rivers in which it was caught: saying often, *That charity gave life to Religion*: and at his return to his house would praise God he had spent that day free from worldly trouble; both harmlessly, and in a rec-reation that became a Church-man. And this good man was well content, if not desirous, that posterity should know he was an Angler, as may appear by his Picture, now to be seen, and carefully kept in *Brase-nose Colledge* (to which he was a liberall benefactor), in which Picture he is drawn leaning on a Desk with his Bible before him, and on one hand of him his *lines, hooks,* and other *tackling* lying in a round; and on his other hand is his Angle-rods of several sorts; and by them this is written, *That he died*. 13 *Feb*. 1601. *being aged*. 95. *years,* 44. *of which he had been Dean of St. Pauls Church; and that his age had neither impair'd his hearing, nor dimm'd his eyes, nor weakn'd his memory, nor made any of the faculties of his mind weak or uselesse.* 'Tis said that *angling* and *temperance* were great causes of these blessings, and I wish the like to all that imitate him, and love the memory of so good a man.

My next and last example shall be that undervaluer of money, the late Provost of *Eton* Colledge, Sir *Henry Wotton* (a man with whom I have often fish'd and convers'd), a man whose forreign Imployments, in the service of this *Nation,* and whose *experience, learning, wit* and *chearfulness* made his company to be esteemed one of the delights of mankind; this man, whose very approbation of angling were sufficient to convince any modest censurer of it, this man was also a most dear lover, and a frequent practiser of the art of angling; of which he would say, '*Twas an imployment for his idle time, which was then not idlely spent*: for angling was after tedious Study, *a rest to his mind, a cheerer of his spirits, a diverter of sadnesse, a calmer of unquiet thoughts, a moderator of passions, a procurer of contentednesse*; and *that it begot habits of* peace *and* patience *in those that profess'd and practis'd it.* Indeed, my friend, you will find angling to be like the vertue of Humility, which has a calmness of spirit, and a world of other blessings attending upon it.

Sir, this was the saying of that learned man, and I do easily believe that *peace,* and *patience,* and a calme *content* did cohabit in the cheerful heart of Sir *Henry Wotton,* because I know that when he was beyond seventy years of age, he made this description of a part of the present pleasure that possess'd him, as he sate quietly in a Summers evening on a bank a Fishing; it

is a description of the Spring, which, because it glides
as soft and sweetly from his pen, as that river does at
this time by which it was then made, I shall repeat it
unto you.

This day dame Nature seem'd in love:
The lusty sap began to move;
Fresh juice did stir th' imbracing Vines,
And birds had drawn their valentines,
The jealous Trout, *that low did lie,*
Rose at a well-dissembled flie;
There stood my friend with patient skill,
Attending of his trembling quill.
Already were the eaves possest
With the swift Pilgrims *dawbed nest:*
The Groves already did rejoyce,
In Philomels *triumphing voice:*
The showers were short, the weather mild,
The morning fresh, the evening smil'd.

   Jone *takes her neat-rub'd pail, and now*
She trips to milk the sand-red Cow;
Where, for some sturdy foot-ball Swain,
Jone *strokes a* sillibub *or twain.*
The fields and gardens were beset
With Tulips, Crocus, Violet,
   And now, though late, the modest Rose
   Did more than half a blush disclose.
   Thus all looks gay, and full of cheer,
   To welcome the new-livery'd year.

These were the thoughts that then possest the undisturbed mind of Sir *Henry Wotton*. Will you hear the wish of another Angler, and the commendation of his happy life which he also sings in Verse? *viz.* Jo. *Davors* Esq.

Let me live harmlessly, and near the brink
   Of Trent *or* Avon *have a dwelling place;*
Where I may see my quill or cork *down sink*
   With eager bit of Pearch, *or* Bleak, *or* Dace;
And on the world and my Creator think,
   Whilst some men strive, ill gotten goods t' imbrace;
And others spend their time in base excesse
Of wine or worse, in war *and* wantonness.

Let them that list, these pastimes still pursue,
   And on such pleasing fancies feed their fill,
So I the fields *and* Meadowes *green may view,*
   And daily by fresh Rivers *walk at will,*
Among the Daisies *and the* Violets *blue.*
   Red Hiacynth, *and yellow* Daffadil,
Purple Narcissus *like the morning rayes,*
Pale Gandergrasse, *and azure* Culverkayes.

I count it higher pleasure to behold
   The stately compasse of the lofty skie,
And in the midst thereof (like burning gold)
   The flaming Chariot of the worlds great eye,
The watry cloudes that in the air up rold,
   With sundry kinds of painted colours flie;
And fair Aurora lifting up her head,
Still blushing, rise from old Tithonius *bed.*

*T*he hills *and* mountains *raised from the* plains,
  *T*he plains *extended level with the* ground,
*T*he grounds *divided into sundry vains,*
  *T*he veins *inclos'd with* rivers *running round;*
*T*hese rivers *making way through natures chains*
  *W*ith *headlong course, into the sea profound;*
*T*he raging sea, beneath the vallies low,
*W*here lakes *and* rils *and* rivulets *do flow.*

*T*he lofty woods, the forrests wide and long
  Adorn'd *with leaves and branches fresh and green,*
*I*n *whose cool bowres the birds with many a song*
  *D*o *welcome with their* Quire *the* Summers Queen;
*T*he Meadowes *fair, where* Flora's *gifts among*
  Are *intermixt, with verdant grasse between.*
*T*he silver-scaled fish that softly swim
*W*ithin *the sweet brooks crystal watry stream.*

*A*ll *these, and many more of his* Creation,
  *T*hat *made the* Heavens, *the* Angler *oft doth see,*
*T*aking *therein no little delectation,*
  *T*o *think how strange, how wonderful they be;*
*F*raming *thereof an inward contemplation,*
  *T*o *set his heart from other fancies free;*
*A*nd *whilst he looks on these with joyful eye,*
*H*is *mind is wrapt above the starry* Skie.

Sir I am glad my memory has not lost these last
Verses, because they are somewhat more pleasant and
more sutable to *May-Day,* then my harsh Discourse:
and I am glad your patience hath held out so long, as

to hear them and me: for both together have brought us within the sight of the T*hatcht* house: and I must be your Debtor (if you think it worth your attention) for the rest of my promised discourse, till some other opportunity, and a like time of leisure.

VENA. Sir, you have Angled me on with much pleasure to the T*hatcht house*: and I now find your words true T*hat good company makes the way seem short,* for trust me, Sir, I thought we had wanted three miles of this H*ouse* till you shewed it to me: but now we are at it, we'l turn into it, and refresh our selves with a cup of drink and a little rest.

PISC. Most gladly (Sir) and we'l drink a civil cup to all the O*tter Hunters* that are to meet you to morrow.

VENA. That we will Sir, and to all the lovers of Angling too, of which number, I am now willing to be one my self, for by the help of your good discourse and company, I have put on new thoughts both of the Art of Angling, and of all that professe it: and if you will but meet me to morrow at the time and place appointed, and bestow one day with me and my friends in hunting the O*tter,* I will dedicate the next two dayes to wait upon you, and we two will for that time do nothing but angle, and talk of fish and fishing.

PISC. 'Tis a match, Sir, I'l not fail you, God willing, to be at A*mwel-hill* to-morrow morning before Sun-rising.

Observations of the Otter and Chub.

Vena. My friend *Piscator*, you have kept time with my thoughts, for the Sun is just rising, and I my self just now come to this place, and the dogs have just now put down an *Otter*; look down at the bottom of the hill there in that Meadow, chequered with *water-Lillies* and *Lady-smocks,* there you may see what work they make; look looke, you may see all busie, men and dogs, dogs and men, all busie.

Pisc. Sir, I am right glad to meet you, and glad to have so fair an entrance into this dayes sport, and glad to see so many dogs, and more men all in pursuit of the *Otter*; lets complement no longer, but joyn unto them; come honest Venator, lets be gone, lets make hast, I long to be doing: no reasonable hedge or ditch shall hold me.

Vena. Gentleman Hunts-man where found you this *Otter*?

Hunt. Marry (Sir) we found her a mile from this place a fishing; she has this morning eaten the greatest part of this *Trout*; she has only left thus much of it as you see, and was fishing for more: when we came we found him just at it: but we were here very early, we were here an hour before Sun-rise, and have given her no rest since we came, sure she'l hardly escape all these dogs and men. I am to have the skin if we kill him.

VENA. Why, Sir, what's the skin worth?

HUNT. 'Tis worth ten shillings to make gloves; the gloves of an *Otter* are the best fortification for your hands that can be thought on against wet weather.

PISC. I pray, honest Huntsman, let me ask you a pleasant question, do you hunt a beast or a fish?

HUNT. Sir, it is not in my power to resolve you, I leave it to be resolved by the Colledge of *Carthusians,* who have made vows never to eat flesh. But I have heard, the question hath been debated among many great Clerks, and they seem to differ about it; yet most agree that his tail is Fish: and if his body be Fish too, then I may say, that a Fish will walk upon land (for an *Otter* does so) sometimes five or six, or ten miles in a night. But (Sir) I can tell you certainly, that he devours much Fish, and kills and spoils much more than he eats: And I can tell you, that this Dog-fisher (for so the Latins call him) can smell a Fish in the water an hundred yards from him (*Gesner* sayes, much farther) and that his stones are good against the Falling-sickness: and that there is an herb *Benione,* which being hung in a linnen cloth near a Fish-pond, or any haunt that he uses, makes him to avoid the place; which proves he smels both by water and land: and I can tell you there is brave hunting this Water-dog in *Cornwall,* where there have been so many, that our *Cambden* sayes, there is a River called *Ottersey,* which was so named, by reason of the abundance of *Otters* that bred and fed in it.

And thus much for my knowledge of the *Otter,* which you may now see above water at vent, and the dogs close with him; I now see he will not last long, follow therefore my Masters, follow, for *Sweetlips* was like to have him at this vent.

VENA. Oh me, all the Horse are got over the River, what shall we do now? shall we follow them over the water?

HUNT. No, Sir, no, be not so eager, stay a little and follow me, for both they and the dogs will be suddenly on this side again, I warrant you: and the *Otter* too, it may be: now have at him with *Kilbuck,* for he vents again.

VENA. Marry so he is, for look he vents in that corner. Now, now *Ringwood* has him: now he's gone again, and has bit the poor dog. Now *Sweetlips* has her: hold her *Sweetlips!* now all the dogs have her, some above and some under water; but now, now she's tir'd, and past losing: come bring him to me, *Sweetlips.* Look, 'tis a Bitch-*Otter,* and she has lately whelp'd, let's go to the place where she was *put down*; and not far from it you will find all her young ones, I dare warrant you, and kill them all too.

HUNT. Come, Gentlemen, come all, let's go to the place where we *put down* the Otter. Look you, hereabout it was that she kennell'd; look you, here it was indeed, for here's her young ones, no less than five; come let's kill them all.

PISC. No, I pray Sir, save me one, and I'll try if I can make her tame, as I know an ingenuous Gentleman in *Leicester shire* (Mr. *Nich. Seagrave*) has done; who hath not onely made her tame, but to catch Fish, and do many other things of much pleasure.

HUNT. Take one with all my heart, but let us kill the rest. And now let's go to an honest Ale-house, where we may have a cup of good *Barley-wine,* and sing *Old Rose,* and all of us rejoyce together.

VENA. Come my friend, *Piscator,* let me invite you along with us; I'll bear your charges this night, and you shall bear mine to morrow; for my intention is to accompany you a day or two in Fishing.

PISC. Sir, your request is granted, and I shall be right glad, both to exchange such a courtesie, and also to enjoy your company.

VENA. Well, now let's go to your sport of Angling.

PISC. Let's be going with all my heart. God keep you all, Gentlemen, and send you meet this day with another Bitch-Otter, and kill her merrily, and all her young ones too.

VENA. Now, *Piscator,* where will you begin to fish?

PISC. We are not yet come to a likely place, I must walk a mile further yet, before I begin.

VENA. Well then, I pray, as we walk tell me freely, how do you like mine Hoste and the company? is not mine Hoste a witty man?

PISC. Sir, I will tell you presently what I think of your Hoste; but first I will tell you, I am glad these *Otters* were killed, and I am sorry there are no more

Otter-killers: for I know that the want of *Otter-killers*, the not keeping the *Fence-moneths* for the preservation of *fish*, will in time prove the destruction of all *rivers*; and those very few that are left that make conscience of the Laws of the Nation, and of keeping dayes of abstinence, will be forced to eat flesh, or suffer more inconveniencies than is yet foreseen.

VENA. Why Sir, what be those that you call the Fence-moneths?

PISC. Sir, they be principally three, namely, *March, April,* and *May,* these being the usual moneths that *Salmon* come out of the Sea to spawn in most fresh Rivers, and their Fry would about a certain time return back to the salt water, if they were not hindred by *weres* and *unlawful gins,* which the greedy Fishermen set, and so destroy them by thousands, as they would (being so taught by nature) change the *fresh* for *salt water.* He that shall view the wise Statutes made in the 13. of E*dw. the* I. and the like in R*ich. the* III. may see several provisions made against the destruction of Fish: and though I profess no Knowledge of the Law, yet I am sure the regulation of these defects might be easily mended. But I remember that a wise friend of mine did usually say, T*hat which is everybodies business is no bodies business.* If it were otherwise, there could not be so many Nets and Fish that are under the Statute size sold daily amongst us, and of which the *conservators* of the waters should be ashamed.

But above all, the taking Fish in Spawning-time,

may be said to be against nature; it is like taking the dam on the nest when she hatches her young: a sin so against nature, that Almighty God hath in holy Writ made a Law against it.

But the poor Fish have enemies enough besides such unnatural *Fisher-men,* as namely, the *Otters* that I spake of, the *Cormorant,* the *Bitterne,* the *Osprey,* the *Sea-gull,* the *Herne,* the *King-fisher,* the *Gorrara,* the *Puet,* the *Swan, Goose, Ducks,* and the *Craber,* which some call the Water-rat: against all which any honest man may make a just quarrel, but I will not, I will leave them to be quarrelled with, and kil'd by others; for I am not of a cruel nature, I love to kill nothing but Fish.

And now to your question concerning your Hoste, to speak truly, he is not to me a good companion: for most of his conceits were either Scripture-jests, or lascivious jests; for which I count no man witty; for the Devil will help a man that way inclined to the first, and his own corrupt nature (which he alwayes carries with him) to the latter. But a companion that feasts the company with *wit* and *mirth,* and leaves out the sin (which is usually mixt with them) he is the man; and indeed such a companion should have his charges borne: and to such company I hope to bring you this night; for at *Trout-Hall,* not far from this place, where I purpose to lodge to night, there is usually an angler that proves good company: and let me tell you, good company and good discourse are the very sinews of vertue: but for such discourse as we heard last night, it infects others, the very boyes will learn to talk and swear as they heard mine Host, and another of the company that shall be nameless; I am sorry he is a Gentleman, for lesse Religion will not save their souls than a beggars; I think more will be required at the last great day. Well, you know what Example is able to do, and I know what the Poet sayes in the like case, which is worthy to be noted by all parents and people of civility:

> ——*Many a one*
> *Owes to his Country his Religion:*
> *And in another would as strongly grow,*
> *Had but his nurse or mother taught him so.*

This is reason put into Verse, and worthy the consideration of a wise man. But of this no more, for though I love civility, yet I hate severe censures: I'll to my own art; and I doubt not but at yonder tree I shall catch a *Chub,* and then we'l turn to an honest cleanly Hostess, that I know right well; rest our selves there, and dress it for our dinner.

VENA. Oh *Sir,* a *Chub* is the worst Fish that swimmes, I hoped for a *Trout* to my dinner.

PISC. Trust me, Sir, there is not a likely place for a *Trout,* hereabout, and we staid so long to take our leave of your Huntsmen this morning, that the Sun is got so high, and shines so clear, that I will not undertake the catching of a *Trout* till evening; and though a *Chub* be by you and many others reckoned the worst of *fish,* yet you shall see I'll make it a good Fish, by dressing it.

VENA. Why, how will you dresse him?

PISC. I'll tell you when I have caught him. Look you here, Sir, do you see? (but you must stand very close) there lye upon the top of the water in this very hole twenty *Chubs,* I'll catch onely one, and that shall be the biggest of them all: and that I will do so, I'll hold you twenty to one, and you shall see it done.

VENA. I marry Sir, now you talk like an Artist, and I'll say you are one, when I shall see you perform what you say you can do; but I yet doubt it.

PISC. You shall not doubt it long, for you shall see me do it presently: look, the biggest of these *Chubs* has had some bruise upon his tail, by a Pike or some other accident, and that looks like a white spot; that very *Chub* I mean to put into your hands presently; sit you but down in the shade, and stay but a little while, and I'le warrant you, I'le bring him to you.

VENA. I'le sit down and hope well, because you seem to be so confident.

PISC. Look you Sir, there is a tryal of my skill, there he is, that very *Chub* that I shewed you with the white spot on his tail; and I'le be as certain to make him a good dish of meat, as I was to catch him. I'le now lead you to an honest Ale-house where we shall find a cleanly room, *Lavender* in the Windows, and twenty *Ballads* stuck about the wall; there my Hostis (which I may tell you, is both cleanly, and handsome, and civil) hath drest many a one for me, and shall **now** dresse it after my fashion, and I warrant it good meat.

VENA. Come Sir, with all my heart, for I begin to be hungry, and long to be at it, and indeed to rest myself too; for though I have walk'd but four miles this morning, yet I begin to be weary; yesterdayes hunting hangs still upon me.

PISC. Well Sir, and you shall quickly be at rest, for yonder is the house I mean to bring you to.

Come Hostis, how do you? Will you first give us a cup of your best drink, and then dress this *Chub,* as you drest my last, when I and my friend were here about eight or ten dayes ago? but you must do me one courtesie, it must be done instantly.

HOST. I will do it, Mr. *Piscator,* and with all the speed I can.

PISC. Now Sir, has not my Hostis made hast? and does not the fish look lovely?

VENA. Both, upon my word, Sir, and therefore let's say grace and fall to eating of it.

PISC. Well Sir, how do you like it?

VENA. Trust me, 'tis as good meat as I ever tasted: now let me thank you for it, drink to you, and beg a courtesie of you; but it must not be deny'd me.

PISC. What is it I pray Sir? you are so modest, that me thinks I may promise to grant it before it is ask'd.

VENA. Why Sir, it is that from henceforth you will allow me to call you *Master,* and that really I may be your Scholar, for you are such a companion, and have so quickly caught, and so excellently cook'd this fish, as makes me ambitious to be your Scholar.

PISC. Give me your hand; from this time forward I will be your Master, and teach you as much of this Art as I am able; and will, as you desire me, tell you somewhat of the nature of most of the Fish that we are to Angle for, and I am sure I both can and will tell you more than any common *Angler* yet knows.

How to fish for, and to dresse the Chavender *or* Chub.

Pisc. The *Chub,* though he eat well thus drest, yet as he is usually drest, he does not: he is objected against, not onely for being full of small forked bones, disperst through all his body, but that he eats watrish, and that the flesh of him is not firm, but short and tastelesse. The French esteem him so mean, as to call him U*n villain*; nevertheless he may be so drest as to make him very good meat; as namely, if he be a large Chub, then dress him thus:

First scale him, and then wash him clean, and then take out his guts; and to that end make the hole as little and near to his gills as you may conveniently, and especially make clean his throat from the grass and weeds that are usually in it (for if that be not very clean, it will make him to taste very sour); having so done, put some sweet herbs into his belly, and then tye him with two or three splinters to a spit, and rost him, basted often with vinegar, or rather verjuice and butter, with good store of salt mixt with it.

Being thus drest, you will find him a much better dish of meat than you, or most folk, even than Anglers themselves do imagine; for this dries up the fluid watry humor with which all *Chubs* do abound.

But take this rule with you, That a *Chub* newly taken and newly drest, is so much better than a *Chub* of a days keeping after he is dead, that I can compare him to nothing so fitly as to Cherries newly gathered from a tree, and others that have been bruised and layen a day or two in water. Being thus used and drest presently, and not washt after he is gutted, (for note that lying long in water, and washing the blood out of the Fish after they be gutted, abates much of their sweetnesse) you will find the Chub to be such meat as will recompence your labour.

Or you may dress the *Chavender* or *Chub* thus:

When you have scaled him, and cut off his tail and fins, and washed him very clean, then chine or slit him through the middle, as a salt fish is usually cut, then give him three or four cuts or scotches with your knife, and broil him on Char-coal, or Wood-coal that are free from smoke, and all the time he is a-broyling baste him with the best sweet butter, and good store of salt mixt with it; and to this add a little Time cut exceeding small, or bruised into the butter. The Cheven thus drest hath the watry taste taken away, for which so many except against him. Thus was the Cheven drest that you liked so well, and commended so much. But note again, that if this Chub that you eat of had been kept till to morrow, he had not been worth a rush. And remember that his throat be very clean, I say very clean, and his body not washt after he is gutted.

Well Scholar, you see what pains I have taken to recover the lost credit of the poor despised *Chub*. And now I will give you some rules how to catch him; and I am glad to enter you into the Art of fishing by catching a *Chub*, for there is no Fish better to enter a young Angler, he is so easily caught, but then it must be this particular way.

Go to the same hole in which I caught my *Chub*, where, in most hot dayes you will find a dozen or twenty Chevens floating near the top of the water, get two or three Grashoppers as you go over the meadow, and get secretly behind the tree, and stand as free from motion as is possible, then put a Grashopper on your hook, and let your hook hang a quarter of a yard short of the water, to which end you must rest your rod on some bough of the tree, and it is likely the Chubs will sink down towards the bottom of the water at the shadow of your Rod (for a Chub is the fearfullest of fishes,) and will do so if but a bird flies over him, and makes the least shadow on the water: but they will presently rise up to the top again, and there lie soaring till some shadow affrights them again: when they lie upon the top of the water, look out the best Chub, which you setting your self in a fit place, may very easily see, and move your Rod as softly as a Snail moves, to that Chub you intend to catch; let your bait fall gently upon the water three or four inches before him, and he will infallibly take the bait, and you will be as sure to catch him: for he is one of the leather-mouth'd Fishes, of which a hook does scarce ever lose his hold: and therefore give him play enough before you offer to take him out of the water. Go your way presently, take my Rod, and do as I bid you, and I will sit down and mend my tackling till you return back.

VENA. Truly, my loving Master, you have offered me as fair as I could wish. I'le go and observe your directions.

Look you, Master, what I have done, that which joies my heart, caught just such another *Chub* as yours was.

PISC. Marry, and I am glad of it: I am like to have a towardly Scholar of you. I now see, that with advice and practice you will make an *Angler* in a short time. Have but a love to it and I'le warrant you.

VENA. But Master, What if I could not have found a *Grashopper?*

PISC. Then I may tell you, that a *black snail,* with his belly slit, to show his white; or a piece of soft *cheese,* will usually do as well: nay, sometimes a *worm,* or any kind of *fly,* as the *Ant-fly,* the *Flesh-fly,* or *Wall-fly,* or the *Dor* or *Beetle* (which you may find under a *Cow-tird*) or a *Bob,* which you will find in the same place, and in time will be a Beetle, it is a short white worm, like to, and bigger than a Gentle, or a *Cod-worm,* or a *Case-worm,* any of these will do very well to Fish in such a manner. And after this manner you may catch a *Trout* in a hot evening: when as you walk by a Brook, and shall see or hear him leap at flies, then if you get a *Grashopper,* put it on your hook, with your line about two yards long, standing behind a bush or tree where his hole is, and make your bait stir up and down on the top of the water; you may, if you stand close be sure of a bite, but not sure to catch him, for he is not a leather-mouthed Fish: and after this manner you may fish for him with almost any kind of live flie, but especially with a *Grashopper*.

VENA. But before you go further, I pray good Master, what mean you by a leather-mouthed Fish?

PISC. By a leather-mouthed Fish, I mean such as have their teeth in their throat, as the *Chub* or *Cheven*, and so the *Barbel*, the *Gudgeon* and *Carp*, and divers others have; and the hook being stuck into the leather or skin of such Fish does very seldom or never lose its hold: But on the contrary, a *Pike*, a *Pearch*, or *Trout*, and so some other Fish, which have not their teeth in their throats, but in their mouths (which you shall observe to be very full of bones, and the skin very thin, and little of it): I say, of these Fish the hook never takes so sure hold, but you often lose the Fish, unless he have gorg'd it.

VENA. I thank you good Master for this observation; but now what shall be done with my *Chub* or *Cheven*, that I have caught?

PISC. Marry Sir, it shall be given away to some poor body, for I'll warrant you I'll give you a *Trout* for your supper: and it is a good beginning of your Art to offer your first fruits to the poor, who will both thank God and you for it, which I see by your silence you seem to consent to. And for your willingness to part with it so charitably, I will also teach you more concerning Chub-Fishing: you are to note, that in *March* and *April* he is usually taken with wormes; in *May,* and *June,* and *July* he will bite at any *fly,* or at cherries or at *Beetles* with their legs and wings cut off, or at any kind of *Snail,* or at the black *Bee* that breeds in clay walls; and he never refuses a Grashopper on the top of a swift stream, nor at the bottom the young *bumble-bee* that breeds in long grasse, and are ordinarily found by the Mower of it. In *August,* and in the cooler moneths a yellow *paste,* made of the strongest cheese, and pounded in a Morter with a little butter and saffron (so much of it as being beaten small will turn it to a lemmon colour). And some make a paste for the Winter moneths, at which time the Chub is accounted best, for then it is observed, that the forked bones are lost or turned into a kind of gristle, especially if he be baked with a paste made of Cheese and Turpentine; he will bite also at a Minnow or Penk as a Trout will: of which I shall tell you more hereafter, and of divers other baits. But take this for a rule, that in hot weather he is to be fisht for towards the mid-water, or nearer the top; and in colder weather nearer the bottom. And if you fish for him on the top, with a Beetle or any *fly,* then be sure to let your line be very long, and to keep out of sight. And having told you that his Spawn is excellent, and that the head of a large Cheven, the Throat being well washt, is the best part of him, I will say no more of this Fish at the present, but wish you may catch the next you Fish for.

And now my next observation and direction shall be concerning the *Trout* (which I love to angle for above any Fish) but lest you may judge me too nice in urging to have the Chub drest so presently after he is taken, I will commend to your consideration how curious former times have been in the like kind.

You shall read in *Seneca* his natural Questions (*Lib.* 3, *cap.* 17.) that the Ancients were so curious in the newnesse of their Fish, that that seemed not new enough that was not put alive into the guests hand; and he sayes that to that end they did usually keep them living in glass-bottels in their Dining-rooms; and they did glory much in their entertaining of friends to have that Fish taken from under their table alive, that was instantly to be fed upon. And he sayes, they took a great pleasure to see their Mullets change to severall colours, when they were dying. But enough of this, for I doubt I have stayed too long from giving you some observations of the *Trout,* and how to fish for him, which shall take up the next of my spare time.

Observations of the nature and breeding of the Trout, and how to fish for him. And the Milk-maids Song.

Pisc. The *Trout* is a Fish highly valued both in this and forraign Nations; he may be justly said (as the old Poet said of Wine, and we English say of Venison) to be a generous Fish: a Fish that is so like the *Buck*, that he also has his seasons; for it is observed, that he comes in and goes out of season with the *Stag* and *Buck*: *Gesner* sayes, his name is of a Germane off-spring, and sayes he is a Fish that feeds clean and purely, in the swiftest streams, and on the hardest gravel: and that he may justly contend with all fresh-water-Fish, as the Mullet may with all Sea-Fish, for precedency and daintinesse of taste, and that being in right season, the most dainty pallates have allowed pre-cedency to him.

And before I go farther in my Discourse, let me tell you, that you are to observe, that as there be some *barren Does,* that are good in Summer, so there be some *barren Trouts* that are good in Winter, but there are not many that are so; for usually they be in their perfection in the month of *May,* and decline with the *Buck*. Now you are to take notice, that in several Countryes, as in *Germany* and in other parts, compar'd to ours, Fish do differ much in their bignesse, and shape, and other-wayes, and so do *Trouts* it is well known that in the Lake *Lemon* (the Lake of *Geneva*,) there are *Trouts* taken of three Cubits long, as is affirmed by *Gesner,* a Writer of good credit; and *Mercator* sayes, the *Trouts* that are taken in the Lake of *Geneva*, are a great part of the Merchandize of that famous City. And you are further to know, that there be certain waters that breed *Trouts* remarkable, both for their number and smalnesse. I know a little Brook in *Kent,* that breeds them to a number incredible, and you may take them twenty or forty in an hour, but none greater than about the size of a *Gudgion*: There are also in divers Rivers, especially that relate to or be near to the Sea (as *Winchester,* or the *Thames* about *Windsor*), a little *Trout* called a *Samlet* or *Skegger Trout* (in both which places I have caught twenty or forty at a standing) that will bite as fast and as freely as *Minnows*; these be by some taken to be young *Salmons,* but in those waters they never grow to be bigger than a *Herring.*

There is also in Kent near to *Canterbury,* a *trout*: (called there a *Fordidge trout*) a *trout* (that bears the name of the Town, where it is usually caught) that is accounted the rarest of Fish, many of them near the bignesse of a *Salmon,* but known by their different colour, and in their best season cut very white; and none of these have been known to be caught with an Angle, unless it were one that was caught by Sir *George Hastings* (an excellent Angler, and now with

God), and he hath told me, he thought that *trout* bit not for hunger but wantonness; and it is the rather to be believed, because both he then, and many others before him, have been curious to search into their bellies, what the food was by which they lived; and have found out nothing by which they might satisfie their curiosity.

Concerning which you are to take notice, that it is reported by good Authors, that there is a Fish, that hath not any mouth, but lives by taking breath by the porings of her Gills, and feeds and is nourished by no man knows what; and this may be believed of the *Fordidge trout*, which (as it is said of the *Storke*, that he knows his season, so he) knows his times (I think almost his day) of coming first into that River out of the Sea, where he lives (and it is like, feeds) nine months of the Year, and about three in the River of *Fordidge*. And you are to note, that the Townsmen are very punctual in observing the very time of beginning to fish for them; and boast much that their River affords a Trout, that exceeds all others. And just so doth *Sussex* boast of several Fish, as namely a *Shelsey Cockle*, a *Chichester Lobster*, an *Arundel Mullet*, and an *Amerly Trout*.

And now for some confirmation of the *Fordidge* Trout, you are to know that this Trout is thought to eat nothing in the fresh water; and it may be the better believed, because it is well known, that *Swallows* which are not seen to flie in *England* for six months in the Year, (but about *Michaelmas* leave us for a hotter

Climate), yet some of them that have been left behind their fellows, have been found (many thousands at a time) in hollow trees, where they have been observed, to live and sleep out the whole Winter without meat;[1] and so *Albertus* observes that there is one kind of *Frog* that hath her mouth naturally shut up about the end of *August* and that she lives so all the Winter,[2] and though it be strange to some, yet it is known to too many among us to be doubted.

And so much for these *Fordidge trouts,* which never afford an *A*ngler sport, but either live their time of being in the fresh water by their meat formerly gotten in the Sea, (not unlike the *Swallow* or *Frog*) or by the vertue of the fresh water only; or as the birds of *Paradise,* and the *Camelion* are said to live by the *Sun* and the *aire.*

There is also in *Northumberland* a Trout called a *Bull-trout,* of a much greater length and bignesse, than any in these Southern parts: and there is in many Rivers that relate to the Sea, *Salmon-trouts,* as much different from others, both in shape and in their spots, as we see sheep differ one from another in their shape and bignesse, and in the finenesse of their wool: and certainly, as some pastures do breed larger sheep, so do some Rivers, by reason of the ground over which they run, breed larger *trouts.*

Now the next thing that I will commend to your consideration is, that the *trout* is of a more sudden

[1] *View Sir Fra. Bacon, exper.* 899.
[2] *See Topsel of Frogs.*

growth than other Fish: concerning which you are also to take notice, that he lives not so long as the *Pearch* and divers other Fishes do, as Sir *Francis Bacon* hath observed in his History of Life and Death.

And next you are to take notice, that he is not like the *Crocodile,* which if he lives never so long, yet alwayes thrives till his death: but 'tis not so with the Trout; for after he is come to his full growth, he declines in his body, but keeps his bignesse, or thrives onely in his head till his death. And you are to know, that he will about (especially before) the time of his Spawning, get almost miraculously through *Weires,* and *Floud-gates* against the stream, even through such high and swift places as is almost incredible. Next, that the *Trout* usually Spawns about *October* or *November,* but in some Rivers a little sooner or later: which is the more observable, because most other fish Spawn in the Spring or Summer, when the Sun hath warmed both the earth and water, and made it fit for generation. And you are to note, that he continues many months out of season: for it may be observed of the Trout, that he is like the Buck or the Ox, that will not be fat in many months, though he go in the very same pastures that horses do, which will be fat in one month; and so you may observe, that most other Fishes recover strength, and grow sooner fat, and in season then the Trout doth.

And next, you are to note, that till the Sun gets to such a height as to warm the earth and the water, the Trout is sick and lean, and lowsie, and unwholesome:

for you shall in winter find him to have a big head, and then to be lank, and thin, and lean; at which time many of them have sticking on them Sugs, or *Trout* lice, which is a kind of a worm, in shape like a clove or pin, with a big head, and stickes close to him and sucks his moisture; those, I think, the *Trout* breeds himself, and never thrives till he free himself from them, which is till warm weather comes; and then, as he grows stronger, he gets from the dead still water into the sharp streams, and the gravel, and there rubs off these worms or lice, and then, as he grows stronger, so he gets him into swifter and swifter streams, and there lies at the watch for any flie or Minnow, that comes near to him; and he especially loves the *May-flie,* which is bred of the *Cod-worm* or *Caddis*; and these make the trout bold and lusty, and he is usually fatter and better meat at the end of that month, then at any time of the year.

Now you are to know, that it is observed, that usually the best *trouts* are either red or yellow, though some (as the *Fordidge trout*) be white and yet good; but that is not usual: and it is a note observable, that the female *Trout* hath usually a less head, and a deeper body than the male *Trout*; and is usually the better meat: and note that a hogback, and a little head to any fish, either *Trout, Salmon,* or other fish, is a sign that that fish is in season.

But yet you are to note, that as you see some Willows or palm-trees bud and blossom sooner than others do, so some Trouts be in rivers sooner in season; and as some Hollys or Oaks are longer before they cast their leaves, so are some Trouts in some Rivers longer before they go out of season.

And you are to note, that there are severall kinds of Trouts, though they all go under that generall name; just as there be tame and wild *Pigeons,* and of tame there be *Cropers, Carriers, Runts* (and too many to name) which all differ, and so do *Trouts* in their bignesse, shape, and colour; the great Kentish Hens may be an instance compared to other Hens. And doubtlesse there is a kind of small Trout, which will never thrive to be big, that breeds very many more than others do, that be of a larger size; which you may rather believe, if you consider that the little *Wren* and *Titmouse* will have twenty young at a time, when usually the noble *Hawk,* or the Musical *Thrassel* or *Blackbird* exceed not four or five.

And now I shall try my skill to catch a Trout, and at my next walking either this evening, or to morrow morning I will give you direction, how you your self shall fish for him.

VENA. Trust me, Master, I see now it is a harder matter to catch a *Trout* than a *Chub*: for I have put on patience, and followed you these two hours, and not seen a Fish stir, neither at your Minnow nor your Worm.

PISC. Well Scholar, you must indure worse luck sometime, or you will never make a good Angler. But what say you now? there is a *Trout* now, and a good one too, if I can but hold him, and two or three turnes more will tire him: Now you see he lies still, and the sleight is to land him: Reach me that Landing Net: So (Sir) now he is mine own, what say you now? is not this worth all my labour and your patience?

VENA. On my word Master, this is a gallant *Trout,* what shall we do with him?

PISC. Marry e'en eat him to supper: We'll go to my Hostis, from whence we came; she told me, as I was going out of door, that my brother *Peter,* a good Angler and a chearful companion, had sent word he would lodge there to night, and bring a friend with him. My Hostis has two beds, and, I know, you and I may have the best: we'l rejoice with my brother *Peter* and his friend, tell tales, or sing *Ballads,* or make a Catch or find some harmlesse sport to content us, and passe away a little time without offence to God or man.

VENA. A match, good Master, let's go to that house for the linnen looks white, and smells of Lavender, and I long to lie in a pair of sheets that smell so: lets be going, good Master, for I am hungry again with fishing.

PISC. Nay, stay a little good Scholar, I caught my last *Trout* with a Worm, now I will put on a Minnow and trie a quarter of an hour about yonder trees for another, and so walk towards our Lodging. Look you Scholar, thereabout we shall have a bit presently, or not at all: Have with you (Sir!) on my word I have him. Oh it is a great loggerheaded *Chub*; Come, hang him upon that Willow twig, and lets be going. But

turn out of the way a little, good Scholar, towards yon-
der high hedge: We'll sit whilst this shower falls so
gently upon the teeming earth, and gives yet a sweeter
smell to the lovely flowers that adorn these verdant
Meadowes.

Look; under that broad Beech-tree, I sate down,
when I was last this way a fishing, and the birds in the
adjoyning Grove seemed to have a friendly contention
with an Eccho, whose dead voice seemed to live in a
hallow tree, near to the brow of that Primrose-hil, there
I sate viewing the silver-streams glide silently towards
their center, the tempestuous Sea; yet sometimes op-
posed by rugged roots, and pibble stones, which broke
their waves, and turned them into foam: and some-
times I beguil'd time by viewing the harmlesse Lambs,
some leaping securely in the cool shade, whilst others
sported themselvs in the chearful Sun; and saw others
craving comfort from the swoln Udders of their bleat-
ing Dams. As I thus sate these and other sights had
so fully possest my soul with content, that I thought
as the Poet has happily exprest it:

> I *was for that time lifted above earth;*
> *And possest joyes not promis'd in my birth.*

As I left this place, and entred into the next field, a
second pleasure entertained me, 'twas a handsome
milk-maid, that had cast away all care, and sung like a
Nightingale: her voice was good, and the Ditty fitted
for it, 'twas that smooth song, which was made by K*it*.

Marlow, now at least fifty years ago: and the Milk-maids Mother sung an answer to it, which was made by Sir *Walter Raleigh* in his younger dayes.

They were old fashioned Poetry, but choicely good, I think much better than the strong lines that are now in fashion in this criticall age. Look yonder, on my word, yonder they both be a milking again, I will give her the *Chub,* and perswade them to sing those two songs to us.

God speed you good woman, I have been a Fishing, and am going to *Bleak-Hall* to my bed, and having caught more Fish then will sup my self and my friend, I will bestow this upon you and your Daughter; for I use to sell none.

MILK. Marrie, God requite you Sir, and we'l eat it chearfully: and if you come this way a Fishing two months hence, a grace of God I'le give you a sillybub of new Verjuice; in a new made Hay-cock for it, and my *Maudlin* shall sing you one of her best *Ballads,* for she and I both love all *Anglers,* they be such honest, civil, quiet men; in the mean-time will you drink a draught of *Red-Cowes milk,* you shall have it freely.

PISC. No, I thank you, but I pray do us a courtesie that shall stand you and your daughter in nothing, and yet we will think our selves still something in your debt; it is but to sing us a Song, that was sung by your daughter, when I last past over this Meadow, about eight or nine dayes since.

MILK. What Song was it, I pray? was it, *Come Shep-*

heards deck your beards, or, *As at noon* Dulcina *rested*; or, Philida *flouts me*; or, *Chevy Chase?*

PISC. No, it is none of those: it is a Song, that your daughter sung the first part, and you sung the answer to it.

MILK. O, I know it now, I learn'd the first part in my golden age, when I was about the age of my poor daughter; and the latter part, which indeed fits me best now, but two or three years ago, when the cares of the World began to take hold of me: but you shall, God willing, hear them both, and sung as well as we can, for we both love Anglers. Come *Maudlin,* sing the first part to the Gentlemen with a merry heart, and Ile sing the second, when you have done.

The Milk-Maids Song.

Come live with me, and be my Love,
And we will all the pleasures prove
That valleys, groves, or hills, or fields,
Or woods, and steepy mountain yields.

Where we will sit upon the Rocks,
And see the Shepheards feed our flocks,
By shallow Rivers, *to whose falls,*
Melodious birds sing Madrigals.

And I will make thee beds of Roses,
And then a thousand fragrant Poesies,
A Cap of flower, and a Kirtle
Imbroidered all with leaves of mirtle.

A Gown made of the finest wool
Which from our pretty Lambs we pull;
Slippers lin'd choicely for the cold,
With buckles of the purest gold.

A Belt of Straw, and Ivy-buds,
With Coral Clasps and Amber studs:
And if these pleasures may thee move,
Come live with me and be my Love.

Thy silver dishes for thy meat,
As pretious as the gods do eat,
Shall on an Ivory table be
Prepar'd each day for thee and me.

The Shepherds Swains shall dance and sing
For thy delight each May-morning:
If these delights thy mind may move,
Then live with me, and be my Love.

VENA. Trust me, Master, it is a choice Song, and sweetly sung by honest *Maudlin*. I now see it was not without cause, that our good Queen *Elizabeth* did so often wish her self a Milkmaid all the moneth of *May*, because they are not troubled with cares, but sing sweetly all the day, and sleep securely all the night: and without doubt honest, innocent, pretty *Maudlin* does so. I'le bestow Sir *Thomas Overbury's* Milk-maids wish upon her, *That she may dye in the Spring, and have good store of flowers stuck round about her winding sheet.*

The Milk-Maids Mothers Answer.

If all the world and Love were young,
And truth in every Shepherds tongue,
These pretty pleasures might me move
To live with thee, and be thy Love.

But time drives flocks from field to fold
When rivers rage, and rocks grow cold,
Then Philomel *becometh dumb,*
The Rest complains of cares to come.

The flowers do fade, and wanton fields
To wayward Winter reckoning yields.
A honey tongue, a heart of gall,
Is fancies spring, but sorrows fall,

Thy gowns, thy shooes, thy beds of roses,
Thy cap, thy kirtle, and thy poesies,
Soon break, soon wither, soon forgotten,
In folly ripe, in reason rotten.

Thy Belt of Straw, and Ivy-buds,
Thy Coral Clasps, and Amber-studs,
All these in me no means can move
To come to thee, and be thy Love.

What should we talk of dainties then,
Of better meat than's fit for men?
These are but vain: that's onely good
Which God hath blest, and sent for food.

But could Youth last, and love still breed,
Had joyes no date, nor age no need;
Then those delights my mind might move,
To live with thee, and be thy Love.

PISC. Well sung, good Woman, I thank you. I'le give you another dish of Fish one of these dayes, and then beg another Song of you. Come Scholar, let *Maudlin* alone, do not you offer to spoil her voice. Look, yonder comes mine Hostesse to call us to supper. How now? is my *brother* Peter come?

HOST. Yes, and a friend with him, they are both glad to hear that you are in these parts, and long to see you, and are hungry, and long to be at supper.

*More directions how to fish for, and how to make for
the Trout an artificial Minnow and Fly, and
some merriment.*

PISC. Well met Brother *Peter,* I heard you and a friend would lodge here to night, and that hath made me and my friend cast to lodge here too: My friend is one, that would fain be a brother of the *Angle,* he hath been an *Angler* but this day, and I have taught him how to catch a *Chub* by *dapping* with a *Grashopper,* and he hath caught a lusty one of nineteen inches long. But, I pray Brother, who is it, that is your companion?

PET. Brother *Piscator,* my friend is an honest Country-man, and his name is *Coridon,* a most downright, wittie, and merry companion that met me here purposely to eat a *trout,* and to be pleasant, and I have not yet wet my Line since I came from home: but I will fit him to morrow with a *trout* for his breakfast, if the weather be anything like.

PISC. Nay, brother, you shall not delay him so long, for look you, here is a *Trout* will fill six reasonable bellies. Come Hostess, dress it presently, and get us what other meat the house will afford, and give us some of your best *Barley-wine,* the good liquor that our honest Forefathers did use to drink of, which preserved their health, and made them live so long, and to do so many good deeds.

PET. On my word this *Trout* is in perfect season. Come, I thank you, and here is a hearty draught to you, and to all the brothers of the Angle wheresoever they be, and to my young brothers good fortune to morrow: I will furnish him with a Rod, if you will furnish him with the rest of the Tackling, we will set him up and make him a Fisher.

And I will tell him one thing for his incouragement, that his Fortune hath made him happy to be Scholar to such a Master; a Master that knows as much both of the nature and breeding of fish as any man; and can also tell him as well how to catch and cook them, from the *Minnow* to the *Salmon,* as any that I ever met withall.

PISC. Trust me, brother *Peter,* I find my Scholar to be so sutable to my own humour, which is to be free and pleasant, and civilly merry, that my resolution is to hide nothing that I know from him. Believe me, Scholar, this is my resolution; and so here's to you a hearty draught, and to all that love us, and the honest Art of Angling.

VENA. Trust me, good Master, you shall not sow your seed in barren ground, for I hope to return you an increase answerable to your hopes; but however you shall find me obedient, and thankful, and serviceable to my best abilitie.

PISC. 'Tis enough, honest Scholar, come lets to supper. Come my friend *Coridon* this *Trout* looks lovely, it was twentie two inches when it was taken, and the belly of it looked some part of it as yellow as a Marigold, and part of it as white as a lilly: and yet me thinks it looks better in this good sawce.

COR. Indeed honest friend, it looks well, and tastes well, I thank you for it, and so does my friend *Peter,* or else he is to blame.

PET. Yes, and so I do, we all thank you, and when we have supt, I will get my friend *Coridon* to sing you a Song for requital.

COR. I will sing a song, if any body will sing another; else, to be plain with you, I *will sing none*: I am none of those that sing for meat, but for company: I say, 'T*is merry in* H*all,* W*hen men sing all.*

PISC. I'l promise you I'l sing a song, that was lately made at my request, by Mr. *William Basse,* one that hath made the choice songs of the H*unter in his careere,* and of T*om of Bedlam,* and many others of note; and this that I will sing is in praise of Angling.

COR. And then mine shall be the praise of a Country mans life: What will the rest sing of?

PET. I will promise you, I will sing another song in praise of Angling to morrow night, for we will not part till then, but Fish to morrow, and sup together, and the next day every man leave Fishing, and fall to his businesse.

VENA. 'Tis a match, and I will provide you a Song or

a Catch against then too, which shall give some addition of mirth to the company; for we will be civil and merry too.

PISC. 'Tis a match my Masters, lets ev'n say Grace, and turn to the fire, drink the other cup to wet our whistles, and so sing away all sad thoughts.

Come on my Masters, who begins? I think it is best to draw cuts, and avoid contention.

PET. It is a match. Look, the shortest cut fals to *Coridon*.

COR. Well then, I will begin, for I hate contention.

CORIDONS Song.

Oh the sweet contentment
The country-man doth find!
   high trolollie lollie loe
   high trolollie lee.
That quiet contemplation
possesseth all my mind:
   Then care away,
   And wend along with me.

For Courts are full of flattery,
As hath too oft been tri'd;
   high trolollie lollie loe, &c.
The City full of wantonnesse,
and both are full of pride:
   Then care away, &c.

But oh the honest Country-man
Speaks truely from his heart,
 high trolollie lollie loe, &c.
His pride is in his tillage,
his horses, and his cart:
 Then care away, &c.

Our cloathing is good sheep skins,
Gray russet for our wives,
 high trolollie lollie loe, &c.
'Tis warmth and not gay cloathing
that doth prolong our lives:
 Then care away, &c.

The ploughman, though he labor hard,
Yet on the Holy-Day,
 high trolollie lollie loe, &c.
No Emperour *so merrily*
does passe his time away:
 Then care away, &c.

To recompence our tillage,
The Heavens afford us showrs;
 high trolollie lollie loe, &c.
And for our sweet refreshments
the earth affords us bowers:
 Then care away, &c.

The Cuckoe *and the* Nightingale
Full merily do sing,
 high trolollie lollie loe, &c.

And with their pleasant roundelaies
bid welcome to the Spring:
Then care away, &c.

This is not half the happiness
the country man injoyes;
  high trolollie lollie loe, &c.
Though others think they have as much,
Yet he that says so lies:
  Then come away, turn
  Country man with me.

Jo. Chalkhill.

PISC. Well sung *Coridon,* this Song was sung with mettle, and it was choicely fitted to the occasion; I shall love you for it as long as I know you; I would you were a brother of the Angle, for a companion that is chearful, and free from swearing and scurrilous discourse, is worth gold. I love such mirth as does not make friends ashamed to look upon one another next morning; nor men (that cannot well bear it) to repent the money they spend when they be warmed with drink: and take this for a rule, You may pick out such times and such companies, that you may make your selves merrier for a little than a great deal of money; for *'Tis the company and not the charge that makes the feast:* and such a companion you prove, I thank you for it.

But I will not complement you out of the debt that I owe you, and therefore I will begin my Song, and wish it may be as well liked.

The Anglers Song.

As inward love breeds outward talk,
The Hound *some praise, and some the* Hawk;
Some better pleas'd with private sport,
Use Tenis, *some a* Mistress *court:*
          But these delights I neither wish,
          Nor envy, while I freely fish.

W*ho hunts, doth oft in danger ride;*
W*ho* Hawks, *lures oft both far and wide;*
W*ho uses* Games *shall often prove*
A loser; but who falls in love,
          Is fettered in fond Cupids *snare:*
          My Angle breeds me no such care.

Of Recreation there is none
So free as Fishing is alone;
All other pastimes do no lesse
Than mind and body both possesse:
          My hand alone my work can do,
          So I can fish and study too.

I care not, I, to fish in seas,
Fresh rivers best my mind do please,
Whose sweet calm course I contemplate,
And seek in life to imitate:
          In civil bounds I fain would keep,
          And for my past offences weep.

And when the timorous Trout *I wait*
To take, and he devours my bait,
How poor a thing sometimes I find

Will captivate a greedy mind:
    And when none bite, I praise the wise,
    Whom vain allurements ne're surprise.

But yet though while I fish, I fast;
I make good fortune my repast:
And thereunto my friend invite,
In whom I more than that delight:
    Who is more welcome to my dish,
    Than to my angle was my fish,

As well content no prize to take,
As use of taken prize to make:
For so our Lord was pleased when
He Fishers made fishers of men:
    Where (which is in no other game)
    A man may fish and praise his Name.

The first men that our Saviour dear
Did chuse to wait upon him here,
Blest Fishers were, and fish the last
Food was, that he on earth did taste.
    I therefore strive to follow those,
    Whom he to follow him hath chose.

COR. Well sung brother, you have paid your debt in good coine, we Anglers are all beholding to the good man that made this Song. Come Hostess, give us more Ale, and lets drink to him.

And now lets every one go to bed that we may rise early; but first lets pay our reckoning, for I will have nothing to hinder me in the morning, for my purpose is to prevent the Sun-rising.

PET. A match; Come *Coridon,* you are to be my Bed-fellow: I know, brother, you and your Scholar will lie together; but where shall we meet to morrow night? for my friend *Coridon* and I will go up the water towards *Ware.*

PISC. And my Scholar and I will go down towards *Waltam.*

COR. Then lets meet here, for here are fresh sheets that smell of *Lavender,* and I am sure we cannot expect better meat, or better usage in any place.

PET. 'Tis a match. Good night to every body.

PISC. And so say I.

VENA. And so say I.

PISC. Good morrow good Hostess, I see my brother *Peter* is still in bed: Come give my Scholar and me a Morning-drink, and a bit of meat to breakfast, and be sure to get a good dish of meat or two against supper, for we shall come home as hungry as Hawks. Come Scholar, lets be going.

VENA. Well now, good Master, as we walk towards the River give me direction, according to your promise, how I shall fish for a *Trout.*

PISC. My honest Scholar, I will take this very convenient opportunity to do it.

The Trout is usually caught with a *worm* or a *Minnow* (which some call a *Pinke*) or with a *flie, viz.*

either a *natural* or an *artificial* flie: concerning which three I will give you some observations and directions.

And first for Worms: Of these there be very many sorts, some bred onely in the earth, as the *Earth-worm*: others of or amongst Plants, as the *Dug-worm*; and others bred either out of excrements, or in the bodies of living creatures, as in the horns of Sheep or Deer; or some of dead flesh, as the *Magot* or *gentle*, and others.

Now these be most of them particularly good for particular Fishes: but for the *Trout*, the *dew-worm*, (which some also call the *Lob-worm*) and the *Brand-ling* are the chief; and especially the first for a great Trout, and the latter for a less. There be also of *Lob-worms* some called *squirel-tayles*, (a worm that has a red head, a streak down the back and a broad tail) which are noted to be the best, because they are the toughest and most lively, and live longest in the water: for you are to know, that a dead worm is but a dead bait, and like to catch nothing, compared to a lively, quick, stirring worm: and for a *Brandling*, he is usually found in an old dunghil, or some very rotten place near to it: but most usually in Cow-dung, or hogs-dung, rather than horse-dung, which is somewhat too hot and dry for that worm. But the best of them are to be found in the bark of the Tanners which they cast up in heaps after they have used it about their leather.

There are also divers other kinds of worms which for colour and shape alter even as the ground out of which they are got, as the *marsh-worm,* the *tag-tail,* the *stag-worm,* the *dock-worm,* the *oak-worm,* the *gilt-*

tayle, the *twachel* or *lob-worm* (which of all others is the most excellent bait for a *Salmon*) and too many to name, even as many sorts, as some think there be of several hearbs or shrubs, or of several kinds of birds in the air; of which I shall say no more, but tell you, that what worms soever you fish with, are the better for being long kept before they be used; and in case you have not been so provident, then the way to cleanse and scour them quickly, is to put them all night in water, if they be *Lob-worms*, and then put them into your bag with fennel: but you must not put your Brandling above an hour in water, and then put them into fennel for sudden use: but if you have time and purpose to keep them long, then they be best preserved in an earthen pot with good store of *Mosse*, which is to be fresh every three or four dayes in Summer, and every week or eight dayes in Winter: or at least the mosse taken from them, and clean washed, and wrung betwixt your hands till it be dry, and then put it to them again. And when your worms, especially the Brandling begins to be sick, and lose of his bignesse, then you may recover him, by putting a little milk or cream (about a spoonful in a day) into them by drops on the mosse; and if there be added to the cream an egge beaten and boiled in it, then it will both fatten, and preserve them long. And note, that when the *knot,* which is near to the middle of the *brandling* begins to swell, then he is sick, and, if he be not well look'd to, is near dying. And for mosse, you are to note, that there be divers kinds of it, which I could name to you, but will onely tell you, that that which is likest a *Bucks-Horn* is the best, except it be white mosse, which grows on some heaths, and is hard to be found. And note, that in a very dry time, when you are put to an extremity for worms, Walnut-tree leaves squeez'd into water, or salt in Water, to make it bitter or salt and then that water poured on the ground, where you shall see worms are used to rise in the night, will make them to appear above ground presently.

And now, I shall shew you how to bait your hook with a worm, so as shall prevent you from much trouble, and the loss of many a hook too; when you Fish for a *Trout* with a running line: that is to say, when you fish for him by hand at the ground. I will direct you in this as plainly as I can, that you may not mistake.

Suppose it be a big Lob-worm, put your hook into him somewhat above the middle, and out again a little below the middle: having so done, draw your worm above the arming of your hook, (but note that at the entring of your hook it must not be at the head-end of the worm, but at the taile-end of him, that the point of your hook may come out toward the head-end) and having drawn him above the arming of your hook, then put the point of your hook again into the very head of the worm, till it come near to the place where the point of the hook first came out: and then draw back that part of the worm that was above the shank or arming of your hook, and so fish with it. And if you mean to fish with two worms, then put the second on

before you turn back the hooks-head of the first worm;
you cannot lose above two or three worms before you
attain to what I direct you; and having attain'd it, you
will find it very useful, and thank me for it: For you
will run on the ground without tangling.

Now for the M*innow* or P*enk*, he is easily found and
caught in M*arch*, or in A*pril*; for then he appears in
the River, but Nature hath taught him to shelter and
hide himself in the Winter in ditches that be near to
the River, and there both to hide and keep himself
warm in the mud or in the weeds, which rot not so
soon as in a running River, in which place if he were
in Winter, the distempered Floods that are usually in
that season, would suffer him to take no rest, but carry
him head-long to Mills and Weires to his confusion.
And of these M*innows*, first you are to know, that the
biggest size is not the best; and next, that the middle
size and the whitest are the best: and then you are to
know, that your M*innow* must be so put on your hook
that it must turn round when 'tis drawn against the
stream, and that it may turn nimbly, you must put it
on a big-sized hook as I shall now direct you, which is
thus. Put your hook in at his mouth and out at his
gill, then having drawn your hook 2 or 3 inches be-
yond or through his gill, put it again into his mouth,
and the point and beard out at his taile, and then tie
the hook and his taile about very neatly with a white
thred, which will make it the apter to turn quick in the
water: that done pull back that part of your line which
was slack when you put your hook into the M*innow*

the second time: I say pull that part of it back so that it shall fasten the head, so that the body of the *Minnow* shall be almost streight on your hook; this done, try how it will turn by drawing it cross the water or against the stream, and if it do not turn nimbly, then turn the tail a little to the right or left hand, and try again, till it turn quick; for if not, you are in danger to catch nothing, for know that it is impossible that it should turn too quick: And you are yet to know, that in case you want a *Minnow*, then a small *Loch*, or a *Sticklebag*, or any other small fish will serve as well: And you are yet to know, that you may salt, and by that means keep them fit for use three or four days or longer, and that of salt, bay-salt is the best.

And here let me tell you, what many old Anglers know right well, that at some time, and in some waters a *Minnow* is not to be got, and therefore let me tell you, I have (which I will shew to you) an *artificial Minnow*, that will catch a Trout as well as an artificial *Flie,* and it was made by a handsome Woman that had a fine hand, and a live Minnow lying by her: *the mould or body of the Minnow was cloth, and wrought upon or over it thus with a needle: the back of it with very sad French green silk, and paler green silk towards the belly, shadowed as perfectly as you can imagine, just as you see a Minnow; the belly was wrought also with a needle, and it was a part of it white silk, and another part of it with silver thred, the tail and fins were of a quil, which was shaven thin, the eyes were of two little black beads, and the head was so shadowed, and all of it so curiously wrought, and so exactly dissembled, that it would beguile any sharpe sighted Trout in a swift stream. And this Minnow I will now shew you, and if you like it, lend it you, to have two or three made by it, for they be easily carryed about an Angler, and be of excellent use; for note, that a large Trout will come as fiercely at a Minnow, as the highest mettle Hawk doth seize on a Partridge, or a Greyhound on a Hare.* I have been told, that 160 minnows have been found in a Trouts belly, either the Trout had devoured so many, or the Miller that gave it a friend of mine had forced them down his throat after he had taken him.

Now for *Flies,* which is the third bait wherewith Trouts are usually taken. You are to know, that there are as many sorts of Flies as there be of Fruits: I will name you but some of them, as the *dun-flie,* the *stone-flie,* the *red-flie,* the *moor-flie,* the *tawny-flie,* the *shell-flie,* the *cloudy,* or blackish-flie, the *flag-flie,* the *vine-flie:* there be of flies, *Caterpillars,* and *Canker-flies,* and *Bear-flies,* and indeed too many either for me to name or for you to remember: and their breeding is so various and wonderful, that I might easily amaze my self, and tire you in a relation of them.

And yet I will exercise your promised patience by saying a little of the *Caterpillar* or the *Palmer-flie* or *worm,* that by them you may guesse what a work it were in a Discourse but to run over those very many flies, worms, and little living creatures with which the Sun and Summer adorn and beautifie the River banks and Meadows; both for the recreation and contempla-tion of us Anglers, and which (I think) my self enjoy more than any other man that is not of my profession.

Pliny holds an opinion, that many have their birth or being from a dew that in the Spring falls upon the leaves of trees; and that some kinds of them are from a dew left upon herbs or flowers; and others from a dew left upon Colworts or Cabbages: All which kinds of dews being thickned and condensed, are by the Suns generative heat most of them hatch'd, and in three dayes made living creatures; and these of several shapes and colours; some being hard and tough, some smooth and soft; some are horned in their head, some in their tail, some have none: some have hair, some none; some have sixteen feet, some lesse, and some have none, but (as our *Topsel*[1] hath with great diligence observed) those which have none, move upon the earth or upon broad leaves, their mo-tion being not unlike to the waves of the sea. Some of them he also observes to be bred of the Eggs of other Caterpillars, and that those in their time turn to be *Butter-flyes:* and again, that their Eggs turn the fol-lowing yeer to be *Caterpillars.* And some affirm, that every plant has his particular flye or Caterpillar, which it breeds and feeds. I have seen, and may therefore af-firm it: a green Caterpillar, or worm, as big as a small Peascod, which had fourteen legs, eight on the belly, four under the neck, and two near the tail. It was

[1] In *his history of Serpents.*

found on a hedge of Privet, and was taken thence, and
put into a large Box, and a little branch or two of
Privet put to it, on which I saw it feed as sharply as a
dog gnaws a bone: it lived thus five or six daies, and
thrived, and changed the colour two or three times, but
by some neglect in the keeper of it, it then dyed and
did not turn to a flye: but if it had lived, it had doubt-
lesse turned to one of those flies that some call flies of
prey, which those that walk by the Rivers may in Sum-
mer, see fasten on smaller flies, and I think make them
their food. And 'tis observable, that as there be these
flies of prey which be very large, so there be others
very little, created I think onely to feed them, and bred
out of I know not what; whose life, they say, Nature
intended not to exceed an hour, and yet that life is
thus made shorter by other flies, or accident.

'Tis endless to tell you what the curious searchers
into Natures productions have observed of these
Worms and Flies: But yet I shall tell you what *Aldro-*
vandus, our *Topsel,* and others say of the *Palmer-*
worm, or *Caterpillar,* That whereas others content
themselves to feed on particular herbs or leaves, (for
most think those very leaves that gave them life and
shape, give them a particular feeding and nourish-
ment, and that upon them they usually abide) yet he
observes, that this is called a *pilgrim* or *palmer-worm,*
for his very wandring life and various food; not con-
tenting himself (as others do) with any one certain
place for his abode, nor any certain kind of herb or

flower for his feeding; but will boldly and disorderly wander up and down, and not endure to be kept to a diet, or fixt to a particular place.

Nay, the very colour of *Caterpillars* are, as one has observed, very elegant and beautiful: I shall (for a taste of the rest) describe one of them, which I will sometime the next moneth shew you feeding on a Willow-tree, and you shall find him punctually to answer this very description: *His lips and mouth somewhat yellow, his eyes black as* Jet, *his forehead purple, his feet and hinder parts green, his tayl two forked and black, the whole body stain'd with a kind of red spots which run along the neck and shoulder-blade, not unlike the form of* Saint Andrew's *Crosse, or the letter* X, *made thus crosse-wise, and a white line drawn down his back to his tail; all which add much beauty to his whole body.* And it is to me observable, that at a fixed age this *Caterpillar* gives over to eat, and towards Winter comes to be covered over with a strange shell or crust called an *Aurelia,* and so lives a kind of dead life, without eating all the Winter; and (as others of several kinds turn to be several kinds of flies and vermin the Spring following) so this *Caterpillar* then turns to be a *painted Butter-fly.*[1]

Come, come my Scholar, you see the River stops our morning walk, and I will also here stop my discourse, onely as we sit down under this *Honey-suckle* hedge, whilst I look a Line to fit the Rod that our brother *Peter* hath lent you, I shall for a little confirmation of

---

[1] *View Sir* Fra. Bacon *exper.* 728 *and* 90. *in his Natural History.*

what I have said, repeat the observation of *Du Bartas*:[1]

> *God not contented to each kind to give,*
> *And to infuse the vertue generative,*
> *By his wise power made many creatures breed*
> *Of lifelesse bodies without* Venus *deed.*

> *So the cold humor breeds the* Salamander,
> *Who (in effect) like to her births commander,*
> *With child with hundred winters, with her touch*
> *Quencheth the fire though glowing ne're so much.*

> *So in the fire in burning furnace springs*
> *The Fly* Perausta *with the flaming wings;*
> *Without the fire it dyes, in it it joyes,*
> *Living in that which all things else destroyes.*

> [2] *So slow* Boötes *underneath him sees*
> *In th' Icy Islands goslings hatcht of trees,*
> *Whose fruitful leaves falling into the water,*
> *Are turn'd ('tis known) to living fowls soon after.*

> *So rotten planks of broken ships do change*
> *To* Barnacles. O *transformation strange!*
> *'Twas first a green tree, then a broken hull,*
> *Lately a mushrome, now a flying* Gull.

VENA. O my good Master, this morning walk has
been spent to my great pleasure and wonder: but I
pray, when shall I have your direction how to make
artificial flies, like to those that the *Trout* loves best?
and also how to use them?

[1] 6. Day of Du Bartas.
[2] View Gerh. Herbal and Cambden.

Pisc. My honest Scholar, it is now past five of the Clock, we will fish till nine, and then go to breakfast: Go you to yonder *Sycamore-tree,* and hide your Bottle of drink under the hollow root of it; for about that time, and in that place, we will make a brave breakfast with a piece of powdered Beef, and a Radish or two that I have in my Fish-bag; we shall, I warrant you, make a good, honest, wholsome, hungry breakfast, and I will give you direction for the making and using of your flies: and in the mean time there is your Rod and Line, and my advice is, that you fish as you see me do, and lets try which can catch the first Fish.

Vena. I thank you, Master, I will observe and practice your direction as far as I am able.

Pisc. Look you, Scholar, you see I have hold of a good Fish: I now see it is a Trout. I pray, put that Net under him, and touch not my line, for if you do, then we break all. Well done Scholar, I thank you.

Now for another. Trust me I have another bite: come Scholar, come lay down your Rod, and help me to land this as you did the other. So, now we shall be sure to have a good dish of fish for supper.

Vena. I am glad of that; but I have no fortune: sure, Master, yours is a better Rod, and better tackling.

Pisc. Nay, then take mine, and I will fish with yours. Look you, Scholar, I have another; come, do as you did before. And now I have a bite at another: Oh me! he has broke all; there's half a line and a good hook lost.

Vena. Master, I can neither catch with the first nor second Angle: I have no fortune.

PISC. Look you, Scholar, I have yet another: and now having caught three brace of Trouts, I will tell you a short Tale as we walk towards our breakfast: A *Scholar (a Preacher I should say) that was to preach to procure the approbation of a Parish, that he might be their Lecturer, had got from his Fellow-pupil the copy of a Sermon that was first preached with a great commendation by him that composed and preach'd it; and though the borrower of it preach'd it word for word, as it was at first, yet it was utterly disliked as it was preached by the second: which the sermon-borrower complained of to the lender of it, and was thus answered;* I lent you indeed my Fiddle, *but not my* Fiddlestick; *for you are to know, that every one cannot make musick with my words, which are fitted for my own mouth.* And so, my Scholar, you are to know, that as the ill pronunciation or ill accenting of words in a Sermon spoils it, so the ill carriage of your line, or not fishing even to a foot in a right place, makes you lose your labour: and you are to know, that though you have my F*iddle,* that is, my very Rod and Tacklings with which you see I catch Fish; yet you have not my F*iddlestick,* that is, you yet have not skill to know how to carry your hand and line, nor how to guide it to a right place: and this must be taught you (for you are to remember I told you, Angling is an Art) either by practice, or a long observation, or both. But take this for a rule, when you fish for a Trout with a Worm, let your line have so much, and not more Lead than will fit the stream in which you fish;

that is to say, more in a great troublesome stream than in a smaller that is quieter; as near as may be, so much as will sink the bait to the bottom, and keep it still in motion, and not more.

But now lets say Grace, and fall to breakfast: what say you, Scholar, to the providence of an old Angler? does not this meat taste well? and was not this place well chosen to eat it? for this Sycamore-tree will shade us from the Suns heat.

VENA. All excellent good, and my stomach excellent good too. And I now remember and find that true which devout *Lessius* sayes, *That poor men, and those that fast often, have much more pleasure in eating than rich men and gluttons, that alwayes feed before their stomachs are empty of their last meat, and so rob themselves of that pleasure that hunger brings to poor men.* And I do seriously approve of that saying of yours, *That you had rather be a civil well-grounded, temperate poor Angler, than a drunken Lord.* But I hope there is none such; however I am certain of this, that I have been at many very costly dinners that have not afforded me half the content that this has done, for which I thank God and you.

And now good Master, proceed to your promised direction for making and ordering my Artificial flie.

PISC. My honest Scholar, I will do it, for it is a debt due unto you by my promise: and because you shall not think your self more engaged to me than indeed you really are, I will freely give you such directions as were lately given to me by an ingenuous brother of the

Angle, an honest man, and a most excellent *Flie-fisher*.

You are to note, that there are twelve kinds of Artificial made Flies to Angle with upon the top of the water, (note by the way, that the fittest season of using these is in a blustering windie day, when the waters are so troubled that the natural flie cannot be seen, or rest upon them). The first is the *dun-flie* in *March*, the body is made of *dun wool*, the wings of the Partridges feathers. The second, is another *dun-fly*, the body of B*lack wool*, and the wings made of the black Drakes feathers, and of the feathers under his taile. The third is the *stone-fly* in April, the body is made of *black wool* made yellow under the wings, and under the taile, and so made with wings of the Drake. The fourth is the *ruddy-fly* in the beginning of *May*, the body made of red-wool, wrapt about with black silk, and the feathers are the wings of the Drake, with the feathers of a red Capon also, which hang dangling on his sides next to the tail. The fifth is the *yellow* or *greenish-fly* (in *May* likewise) the body made of *yellow wooll*, and the wings made of the red cocks hackel or tail. The sixth is, the *black-fly* in *May* also, the body made of *black-wool* and lapt about with the herle of a Peacocks tail; the wings are made of the wings of a brown Capon with his blue feathers in his head. The seventh is the sad *yellow-flie* in *June*, the body is made of *black-wool*, with a yellow list on either side, and the wings taken off the wings of a Buzzard, bound with black braked hemp. The eighth is the *moorish-fly* made with the body of duskish wooll, and the wings made of the blackish mail of the Drake. The ninth is the *tawny-fly,* good until the middle of *June;* the body made of *tawny-wool,* the wings made contrary one against the other, made of the whitish mail of the wild Drake. The tenth is the W*asp-fly* in *July,* the body made of *black wool,* lapt about with yellow silk, the wings made of the feathers of the Drake, or of the Buzzard. The eleventh is the *shell-fly,* good in mid *July,* the body made of greenish wool, lapt about with the herle of a Peacocks tail; and the wings made of the wings of the Buzzard. The twelfth is the dark *Drake-fly,* good in A*ugust,* the body made with *black wool,* lapt about with black silk; his wings are made with the mail of the black Drake, with a black head. Thus have you a Jury of flies likely to betray and condemn all the Trouts in the River.

I shall next give you some other Directions for Flie-fishing, such as are given by Mr. *Thomas Barker,* a Gentleman that hath spent much time in Fishing: but I shall do it with a little variation.

First, let your Rod be light, and very gentle, I take the best to be of two pieces, and let not your Line exceed (especially for three or four links next to the hook) I say, not exceed three or four hairs at the most, though you may Fish a little stronger above in the upper part of your Line: but if you can attain to Angle with one hair, you shall have more rises and catch more Fish. Now you must be sure not to cumber yourself with too long a Line, as most do: and before you begin to Angle, cast to have the wind on your back, and the Sun (if it shines) to be before you, and to Fish down the stream; and carry the point or top of your Rod downward, by which means the shadow of your self, and Rod too will be the least offensive to the Fish, for the sight of any shade amazes the Fish, and spoils your sport, of which you must take a great care.

In the middle of *March* (till which time a man should not in honesty catch a Trout) or in *April,* if the weather be dark, or a little windy or cloudy, the best Fishing is with the *Palmer-worm,* of which I last spoke to you, but of these there be divers kinds, or at least of divers colours, these and the *May-fly* are the ground of all Flie-angling, which are to be thus made.

First, you must arm your hook with the line in the inside of it, then take your Scissers, and cut so much of a brown Malards feather as in your own reason will make the wings of it, you having withal regard to the bignesse or littlenesse of your hook, then lay the out-most part of your feather next to your hook, then the point of your feather next the shank of your hook; and, having so done, whip it three or four times about the hook with the same Silk, with which your hook was armed, and having made the Silk fast, take the hackel of a *Cock* or *Capons* neck, or a *Plovers* top, which is usually better: take off the one side of the feather, and then take the hackel, Silk, or Crewel, Gold or Silver thred, make these fast at the bent of the hook, that is to say, below your arming; then you must take the hackel, the Silver or Gold thred, and work it up to the wings, shifting or still removing your fingers as you turn the Silk about the hook: and still looking at every stop or turn, that your Gold, or what materials soever you make your *Fly* of, do lie right and neatly; and if you find they do so, then when you have made the head, make all fast, and then work your hackel up to the head, and make that fast: and then with a needle or pin divide the wing into two, and then with the arming Silk whip it about cross-waies betwixt the wings, and then with your thumb you must turn the point of the feather towards the bent of the hook, and then work three or four times about the shank of the hook, and then view the proportion, and if all be neat and to your liking, fasten.

I confess, no direction can be given to make a man of a dull capacity able to make a Flie well: and yet I know, this with a little practice will help an ingenuous Angler in a good degree: but to see a Flie made by an Artist in that kind, is the best teaching to make it, and then an ingenuous Angler may walk by the River and mark what Flie fall on the water that day, and catch one of them, if he see the *Trouts* leap at a flie of that kind, and then having alwaies hooks ready hung with him, and having a bag also, alwaies with him with Bears hair, or the hair of a Brown or Sad-coloured Heifer, hackels of a Cock or Capon, several coloured Silk and Crewel to make the body of the flie, the feathers of a Drakes head, black or brown Sheeps wool, or Hogs wool, or hair, thred of Gold and of Silver: Silk of several colours (especially sad coloured to make the flies head:) and there be also other coloured feathers both of little birds and of peckled foul. I say, having those with him in a bag, and trying to make a flie, though he miss at first, yet shall he at last hit it better, even to such a perfection as none can well teach him; and if he hit to make his Flie right, and have the luck to hit also where there is store of *Trouts,* a dark day, and a right wind, he will catch such store of them, as will encourage him to grow more and more in love with the Art of *Fly-making.*

VENA. But my loving master, if any wind will not serve, then I wish I were in *Lapland,* to buy a good wind of one of the honest Witches, that sell so many winds, and so cheap.

PISC. Marry Scholar, but I would not be there, nor indeed from under this tree: for look how it begins to rain, and by the clouds if I mistake not we shall presently have a smoaking showre, and therefore sit close; this *Sycamore-tree* will shelter us: and I will tell you, as they shall come into my mind, more observations of flie-fishing for a Trout.

But first for the wind, you are to take notice, that of the winds the *Southwind* is said to be best. One observes, That

> ——*When the wind is South,*
> *It blowes your bait into a fishes mouth.*

Next to that, the W*est* wind is believed to be the best: and having told you that the *East* wind is the worst, I need not tell you which wind is the best in the third degree: And yet (as *Solomon* observes) that He *that considers the wind shall never sow:* so he that busies his head too much about them (if the weather be not made extream cold by an East wind) shall be a little superstitious: For as it is observed by some, That there is no good Horse of a bad colour; so I have observed that if it be a cloudy day, and not extream cold, let the Wind sit in what corner it will, and do its worst. And yet take this for a rule, that I would willingly fish standing on the Lee-shore: and you are to take notice, that the fish lies or swimmes nearer the bottom, and in deeper water in Winter than in Summer; and also nearer the bottom in any cold day, and then gets nearest the low-side of the water.

But I promised to tell you more of the Flie-fishing for a *Trout,* which I may have time enough to do; for you see it rains M*ay-butter:* First for a *May-flie,* you may make his body with greenish coloured Crewel, or Willowish colour; darkning it in most places with waxed Silk, or rib'd black hair, or some of them rib'd with silver thred; and such Wings for the colour as you see the flie to have at that season; nay, at that very day on the water. Or you may make the Oak-flie with an Orange-tawny and black ground, and the brown of a Mallards feather for the Wings; and you are to know, that these two are most excellent flies, that is, the *May-flie* and the Oak-flie. And let me again tell you, that you keep as far from the water as you can possibly, whether you fish with a flie or worm; and fish down the stream; and when you fish with a flie, if it be possible, let no part of your line touch the water, but your flie only; and be still moving your flie upon the water, or casting it into the water, you your self being also alwayes moving down the stream. Mr. *Barker* commends several sorts of the *Palmer* flies, not onely those rib'd with silver and gold, but others that have their bodies all made of black, or some with red, and a red hackel; you may also make the *Hawthorn-flie,* which is all black, and not big, but very small, the smaller the better; or the *Oak-flie,* the body of which is Orange-colour and black Crewel, with a brown Wing; or a Flie made with a *Peacocks* feather, is excellent in a bright day: You must be sure you want not in your Magazine-bag the *Peacocks* feather, and grounds of such wool and Crewel as will make the Grashopper: and note that usually the smallest flies are best: and note also, that the light flie does usually make most sport in a dark day; and the darkest and least flie in a bright or clear day: and lastly note, that you are to repair upon any occasion to your Magazine-bag, and upon any occasion vary and make them lighter or sadder according to your fancy or the day.

And now I shall tell you, that the fishing with a natural flie is excellent, and affords much pleasure; they may be found thus, the *May-flie* usually in and about that moneth near to the River side, especially against rain; the *Oak-flye* on the butt or body of an *Oak* or *Ash* from the beginning of *May* to the end of *August;* it is a brownish flie, and easie to be so found, and stands usually with his head downward, that is to say, towards the root of the tree: the small black flie, or Hawthorn-flie, is to be had on any Hawthorn bush after the leaves be come forth; with these and a short Line (as I shewed to Angle for a *Chub*) you may dape or dop, and also with a *Grashopper* behind a tree, or in any deep hole, still making it to move on the top of the water, as if it were alive, and still keeping your self out of sight, you shall certainly have sport if there be *Trouts;* yea, in a hot day, but especially in the evening of a hot day.

And now, Scholar, my direction for Flie-fishing is ended with this showre, for it has done raining, and now look about you, and see how pleasantiy that Meadow looks; nay, and the Earth smells as sweetly too. Come, let me tell you what holy Mr. *Herbert* sayes of such dayes and flowers as these, and then we will thank God that we enjoy them, and walk to the River and sit down quietly, and try to catch the other brace of *Trouts.*

> *Sweet day, so cool, so calm, so bright,*
> *The bridal of the earth and skie,*
> *Sweet dews shall weep thy fall to night,*
> > *for thou must die.*
>
> *Sweet Rose, whose hew, angry and brave,*
> *Bids the rash gazer wipe his eye,*
> *Thy root is ever in its grave,*
> > *and thou must dye.*
>
> *Sweet Spring, full of sweet dayes and roses,*
> *A box where sweets compacted lye;*
> *My Musick shewes you have your closes,*
> > *and all must dye.*

Only a sweet and virtuous soul,
Like seasoned Timber never gives,
But when the whole world turns to cole,
          then chiefly lives.

VENA. I thank you, good Master, for your good direction for Flie-fishing, and for the sweet injoyment of the pleasant day, which is so far spent without offence to God or man: and I thank you for the sweet close of your discourse with Mr. *Herberts* Verses, which I have heard loved Angling; and I do the rather believe it, because he had a spirit suitable to Anglers, and to those primitive Christians, that you love, and have so much commended.

PISC. Well my loving Scholar, and I am pleased, to know that you are so well pleased with my direction and discourse.

And since you like these Verses of Mr. *Herberts* so well, let me tell you what a reverend and learned Divine that professes to imitate him (and has indeed done so most excellently) hath writ of our *Book* of *Common-Prayer*, which I know you will like the better, because he is a friend of mine, and I am sure no enemy to Angling.

What? prayer by the book? and common? Yes, why
     not?
          The Spirit of grace,
          And supplication
          Is not left free alone
          For time and place,

But *manner too: to read or speak by rote,*
  Is all alike to him, that prayes
  In's heart, what with his mouth he sayes.

They that in private by themselves alone
                Do pray, may take
                What liberty they please,
                In chusing of the wayes
                Wherein to make
Their souls most intimate affections known
  To him that sees in secret, when
  Th' are most conceal'd from other men.

But he, that unto others leads the way
                In publick prayer,
                Should do it so
                As all that hear may know
                They need not fear
To tune their hearts unto his tongue, and say,
  Amen; nor doubt they were betray'd
  To blaspheme, when they should have pray'd.

Devotion will add Life unto the Letter,
                And why should not
                That which Authority
                Prescribes, esteemed be
                Advantage got?
If th' prayer be good, the commoner the better,
  Prayer in the Churches words, as well
  As sense, of all prayers bears the bell.

Ch. Harvie.

And now, Scholar, I think it will be time to repair to our Angle-rods, which we left in the water, to fish for themselves, and you shall chuse which shall be yours; and it is an even lay, one of them catches.

And let me tell you, this kind of fishing with a dead rod, and laying night-hooks, are like putting money to Use; for they both work for the Owners, when they do nothing but sleep, or eat, or rejoyce, as you know we have done this last hour, and sate as quietly and as free from cares under this *Sycamore,* as *Virgills Tityrus* and his *Meliboeas* did under their broad *Beech-tree:* No life, my honest Scholar, no life so happy and so pleasant, as the life of a well governed *Angler;* for when the *Lawyer* is swallowed up with business, and the *Statesman* is preventing or contriving plots, then we sit on *Cowslip-banks,* hear the birds sing, and possesse ourselves in as much quietnesse as these silent silver streams, which we now see glide so quietly by us. Indeed my good Scholar, we may say of *Angling,* as Dr. *Boteler* said of *Strawberries; Doubtlesse God could have made a better berry, but doubtlesse God never did:* And so (if I might be Judge) *God never did make a more calm, quiet, innocent recreation than* Angling.

Ile tell you Schollar, when I sate last on this *Primrose-bank,* and look'd down these Meadows; I thought of them as *Charles* the Emperour did of the City of *Florence: That they were too pleasant to be look'd on, but onely on Holy-Dayes:* as I then sate on this very grass, I turn'd my present thoughts into verse: 'Twas a wish which Ile repeat to you.

The Anglers Wish.

I *in these flowery Meades wo'd be:*
These Christal streams should solace me;
To whose harmonious bubling noise,
I *with my Angle wo'd rejoice,*
Sit here and see the Turtle-dove,
Court his chaste Mate to acts of love,
Or on that bank feel the West wind
Breathe health and plenty, please my mind
To see sweet dew-drops kisse these flowers,
And then washt off by April-*showers:*
Here hear my Clora *sing*[1] *a song,*
There see a Black-bird feed her young,
Or a Leverock *build her nest;*
Here give my weary spirits rest,
And raise my low pitcht thoughts above
Earth, or what poor mortals love:
   Thus free from Law-suits, and the noise
   Of Princes Courts I wo'd rejoyce.

Or with my Bryan, and a book,
Loyter long dayes near Shawford-*brook;*
There sit by him, and eat my meat,
There see the Sun both rise and set:
There bid good morning to next day,
There meditate my time away:

---

[1] Like Hermit poor.

> *And angle on, and beg to have*
> *A quiet passage to a welcome grave.*

When I had ended this composure, I left this place, and saw a Brother of the Angle sit under that *honysuckle-hedge* (one that will prove worth your acquaintance). I sate down by him, and presently we met with an accidental piece of merriment, which I will relate to you; for it rains still.

On the other-side of this very hedge sate a gang of *Gypsies,* and near to them sate a gang of B*eggars.* The *Gypsies* were then to divide all the money that had been got that week, either by stealing linnen or poultrie, or by Fortune-telling or Legerdemain, or, indeed by any other sleights and secrets belonging to their mysterious Government. And the sum that was got that week proved to be but twenty and some odd shillings. The odd money was agreed to be distributed amongst the poor of their own Corporation; and for the remaining twenty shillings, that was to be divided unto four Gentlemen *Gypsies,* according to their several degrees in their Common-wealth.

And the first or chiefest Gypsie, was to have a third part of the twenty shillings, which all men know is 6*s.* 8*d.*

The second was to have a fourth part of the 20*s.* which all men know to be 5*s.*

The third was to have a fifth part of the 20*s.* which all men know to be 4*s.*

The fourth and last Gipsie was to have a sixth part of the 20*s.* which all men know to be 3*s.* 4*d.*

As for example,

3 times 6*s.* 8*d.* is	.	.	.	20*s.*
And so is 4 times 5*s.*	.	.	.	20*s.*
And so is 5 times 4*s.*	.	.	.	20*s.*
And so is 6 times 3*s.* 4*d.*	.	.	20*s.*

And yet he that divided the money was so very a Gipsie, that though he gave to every one these said sums, yet he kept one shilling of it for himself.

	s.	*d.*
As for example,		
	6	8
	5	0
	4	0
	3	4
make but . . .	19	0

But now you shall know, that when the four Gipsies saw he had got one shilling by dividing the money, though not one of them knew why to demand more, yet like Lords and Courtiers every Gipsie envied him that was the gainer, and wrangled with him, and every one said the *remaining shilling belonged to him:* and so they fell to so high a contest about it, as none that knowes the faithfulness of one Gipsie to another, will easily believe; only we that have lived this last twenty years, are certain that money has been able to do much mischief. However the Gipsies were too wise to go to

Law, and did therefore chuse their choice friends *Rook* and *Shark,* and our late English *Gusman,* to be their Arbitrators and Umpire; and so they left this *Honey-succle hedg,* and went to *Tell fortunes,* and *cheat,* and get more money and lodging in the next Village.

When these were gone, we heard as high a contention amongst the *beggars, Whether it was easiest to rip a Cloak, or to unrip a cloak?* One *beggar* affirmed it was all one. But that was denyed by asking her, *If doing and undoing were all one?* then another said, *'Twas easiest to unrip a cloak,* for that was to let it alone. But she was answered, by asking her, how she unript it, if she let it alone? And she confest her self mistaken. These and twenty such like questions were proposed, and answered with as much beggarly Logick and earnestnesse, as was ever heard to proceed from the mouth of the most pertinacious Schismatick; and sometimes all the Beggars (whose number was neither more nor lesse than the Poets nine Muses) talk'd all together about this ripping and unripping, and none heard what the other said; but at last one beggar crav'd audience, and told them, that old father *Claus,* whom *Ben Johnson* in his *Beggars Bush* created King of their Corporation, was that night to lodge at an Ale-house (called *Catch-her-by-the-way,*) not far from *Waltam-Crosse,* and in the high-rode towards *London;* and he desired them to spend no more time about that and such like questions, but refer all to Father *Claus* at night, and in the mean time draw cuts what song

should be next sung, and who should sing it. They all
agreed to the motion, and the lot fell to her that was
the youngest, and veriest Virgin of the Company, and
she sung *Franck Davisons* Song, which he made forty
years ago, and all the others of the company joined to
sing the burthen with her: the Ditty was this, but first
the burthen.

Bright shines the Sun, play beggars play,
Here's scraps enough to serve to day.

What noise of viols is so sweet
As when our merry clappers ring?
What mirth doth want when beggars meet?
A beggar's life is for a King:
  Eat, drink and play, sleep when we list,
  Go where we will, so stocks be mist.
  Bright shines the Sun, play beggars play,
  here's scraps enough to serve to day.

The world is ours and ours alone,
For we alone have world at will;
We purchase not, all is our own,
Both fields and streets we beggars fill:
  Play beggars play, play beggars play,
  here's scraps enough to serve to day.

A hundred herds of black and white
Upon our Gowns securely feed
And yet if any dare us bite,
He dies therefore as sure as Creed:

Thus beggars Lord it as they please,
And only beggars live at ease:
Bright shines the sun, play beggars play,
Here's scraps enough to serve to day.

VENA. I thank you good Master, for this piece of merriment, and this Song, which was well humoured by the Maker, and well remembred by you.

PISC. But I pray forget not the Ketch which you promised to make against night; for our Country-man, honest *Coridon,* will expect your Ketch and my Song, which I must be forced to patch up; for it is so long since I learnt it, that I have forgot a part of it. But come, now it hath done raining, let's stretch our legs a little in a gentle walk to the River, and try what interest our Angles will pay us for lending them so long to be used by the *Trouts,* lent them indeed like Usurers, for our profit and their destruction.

VENA. Oh me, look you Master, a fish a fish, oh las Master, I have lost her.

PISC. I marry Sir, that was a good fish indeed: if I had had the luck to have taken up that Rod, then 'tis twenty to one, he should not have broke my line by running to the rods end as you suffered him: I would have held him within the bent of my Rod (unlesse he had been fellow to the great *Trout* that is near an ell long, which was of such a length and depth, that he had his picture drawn, and now to be seen at mine Hoste *Rickabies* at the *George* in *Ware*), and it may be, by giving that very great *Trout* the Rod, that is, by casting it to him into the water, I might have caught him at the long run; for so I use alwayes to do when I meet with an overgrown fish, and you will learn to do so too hereafter: for I tell you, Scholar, fishing is an Art, or, at least, it is an Art to catch fish.

VENA. But Master, I have heard, that the great *Trout* you speak of is a *Salmon*.

PISC. Trust me Scholar, I know not what to say to it. There are many Countrey people that believe H*ares* change Sexes every year: And there be very many learned men think so too; for in their dissecting them they find many reasons to incline them to that belief. And whether this were a *Salmon* when he came into the fresh water, and his not returning into the Sea hath altered him to another colour or kind, I am not able to say; but I am certain he hath all the signs of being a Trout, both for his *shape, colour,* and *spots,* and yet many think he is not.

VENA. But Master, will this *Trout* which I had hold of die? for it is like he hath the hook in his belly.

PISC. I will tell you, Scholar, that unless the hook be fast in his very Gorge, he will live, and a little time with the help of the water, will rust the hook, and it will in time wear away: as the gravel doth in the horse hoof, which only leaves a false quarter.

And now Scholar, lets go to my Rod. Look you Scholar, I have a fish too, but it proves a logger-headed *Chub,* and this is not much amiss, for this will pleasure some poor body, as we go to our lodging to meet our

Brother *Peter* and honest *Coridon*. Come, now bait your hook again, and lay it into the water, for it rains again; and we will ev'n retire to the *Sycamore-tree,* and there I will give you more directions concerning Fishing: For I would fain make you an Artist.

VENA. Yes, good Master, I pray let it be so.

PISC. Well Scholar, now we are sate down and are at ease, I shall tell you a little more of *trout*-fishing, because I speak of the *Salmon* (which I purpose shall be next), and then of the *Pike* or *Luce*. You are to know, there is night as well as day-fishing for a *trout,* and that in the night the best *trouts* come out of their holes; and the manner of taking them, is on the top of the water with a great *Lob* or *Garden worm,* or rather two, which you are to fish with in a place where the waters run somewhat quietly (for in a stream the bait will not be so well discerned). I say, in a *quiet* or dead place near to some swift, there draw your bait over the top of the Water, to and fro, and if there be a good *trout* in the hole, he will take it, especially if the night be dark: for then he is bold and lies near the top of the water, watching the motion of any *Frog,* or *Water-Rat* or *Mouse* that swims betwixt him and the skie, these he hunts after, if he sees the water but wrinckle, or move in one of these dead holes, where these great old Trouts usually lie near to their holds: for you are to note, that the great old Trout is both subtil and fearful, and lies close all day, and does not usually stir out of his hold but lies in it as close in the day as the *tim-*

erous hare does in her *form:* for the chief feeding of either is seldome in the day, but usually in the night, and then the great Trout feeds very boldly.

And you must fish for him with a strong Line, and not a little hook, and let him have time to gorge your hook, for he does not usually forsake it, as he oft will in the day-fishing: and if the night be not dark, then Fish so with an *Artificial fly* of a light-colour: nay, he will sometimes rise at a dead *Mouse,* or a piece of cloth, or any thing that seems to swim cross the water; or to be in motion: this is a choice way, but I have not oft used it, because it is void of the pleasures, that such dayes as these, that we two now enjoy, afford an Angler.

And you are to know, that in *Hampshire,* which I think exceeds all *England* for swift, shallow, clear, pleasant Brooks, and store of *Trouts,* they use to catch Trouts in the night, by the light of a Torch or straw, which when they have discovered, they strike with a Trout-speer or other wayes. This kind of way they catch very many, but I would not believe it till I was an eye-witness of it, nor do I like it now I have seen it.

VENA. But Master, do not *Trouts* see us in the night?

PISC. Yes, and hear, and smell too, both then and in the day time; for *Gesner* observes, the *Otter* smells a Fish forty furlongs off him in the water: and that it may be true, seems to be affirmed by Sir *Francis Bacon* (in the eighth Century of his Natural History) who there proves, that waters may be the *Medium* of sounds, by demonstrating it thus, *That if you knock two stones together very deep under the water, those that stand on a bank near to that place may hear the noise without any diminution of it by the water.* He also offers the like experiment concerning the letting an *Anchor* fall by a very long cable or rope on a rock, or the sand within the Sea: and this being so well observed and demonstrated, as it is by that learned man, has made me to believe that *Eeles* unbed themselves, and stir at the noise of the Thunder, and not onely, as some think, by the motion or the stirring of the earth, Which is occasioned by that Thunder.

And this reason of Sir *Francis Bacon* (*Exper.* 792.) has made me crave pardon of one that I laught at, for affirming that he knew *Carps* come to a certain place in a Pond to be fed at the ringing of a Bell, or the beating of a Drum: and it shall be a rule for me to make as little noise as I can when I am fishing, until Sir *Francis Bacon* be confuted, which I shall give any man leave to do.

And, lest you may think him singular in this opinion, I will tell you, this seems to be believed by our learned Doctor *Hackwell,* who (in his *Apology of God's Power and Providence,* f. 360) quotes *Pliny* to report that one of the Emperors had particular Fishponds, and in them several Fish, that appeared and came when they were called by their particular names: and St. *James* tells us (*chap.* 1. *and* 7) that all things in the Sea have been tamed by Mankind. And *Pliny* tells us (*lib.* 9. 35) that *Antonia* the Wife of *Drusus* had a *Lamprey,* at whose gils she hung Jewels or Ear-rings;

and that others have been so tender-hearted, as to shed tears at the death of Fishes, which they have kept and loved. And these Observations, which will to most hearers seem wonderful, seem to have a further confirmation from *Martial* (*lib.* 4 epigr. 30.), who writes thus:

Piscator, fuge, ne nocens, &c.

Angler! *would'st thou be guiltless? then forbear,*
For *these are* sacred fishes *that swim here;*
Who *know their Sovereign, and will lick his hand;*
Than *which none's greater in the worlds command:*
Nay *more, th' have names, and when they called are,*
Do *to their several owners Call repair.*

All the further use that I shall make of this, shall be to advise Anglers to be patient, and forbear swearing, lest they be heard and catch no Fish.

And so I shall proceed next to tell you, it is certain, that certain fields near *Lemster,* a Town in *Herefordshire,* are observed that they make the sheep that graze upon them more fat than the next, and also to bear finer Wool; that is to say, that, that year in which they feed in such a particular pasture, they shall yield finer wool than they did that Year before they came to feed in it, and courser again if they shall return to their former pasture; and again return to a finer wool being fed in the fine-wool ground. Which I tell you, that you may the better believe that I am certain, if I catch a *Trout* in one Meadow, he shall be *white* and *faint,* and very like to be *lowsie;* and as certainly, if I catch a

Trout in the next Meadow, he shall be *strong,* and *red,* and *lusty,* and much better meat: Trust me, Scholar, I have caught many a *Trout* in a particular Meadow, that the very shape and the enamell'd colour of him hath been such, as hath joyed me to look on him; and I have with much pleasure concluded with *Solomon, Everything is beautiful in his season.*

I should by promise speak next of the *Salmon,* but I will by your favour say a little of the *Umber* or *Grayling;* which is so like a *Trout* for his shape and feeding, that I desire I may exercise your patience with a short discourse of him, and the next shall be of the *Salmon.*

CHAPTER VI

Observations of the Umber or Grayling, and directions how to fish for them.

Pisc. The Umber and Grayling are thought by some to differ as the Herring and Pilcher do: But though they may do so in other Nations, I think those in England differ nothing but in their names. Aldrovandas sayes, they be of a Trout kind: and Gesner sayes, that in his Countrey (which is Swisserland) he is accounted the choicest Fish. And in Italy, he is in the moneth of May so highly valued, that he is sold then at a much higher rate than any other Fish. The French (which call the Chub Un Villain) call the Umber of the Lake Lemon, Un Umble Chevaliere; and they value the Umber or Grayling so highly, that they say he feeds on Gold, and that many have been caught out of their famous River of Loyre, out of whose bellies grains of gold have been often taken. And some think that he feeds on Water-time, and smells so at his first taking out of the water; and they may think so with as good reason as we do, that our Smelts smell like Violets at their being first caught; which I think is a truth. Aldrovandus sayes, the Salmon, the Grayling, and Trout, and all Fish that live in clear and sharp streams, are made by their mother Nature of such exact shape

and pleasant colours, purposely to invite us to a joy
and contentednesse in feasting with her. Whether this
is a truth or not, is not my purpose to dispute; but 'tis
certain, all that write of the *Umber* declare him to be
very medicinable. And *Gesner* sayes, that the fat of a
Grayling being set with a little Honey a day or two in
the Sun in a little glass, is very excellent against red-
ness, or any thing that breeds in the eyes. *Salvian* takes
him to be called *Umber* from his swift swimming or
gliding out of sight, more like a shadow or a ghost
than a fish. Much more might be said both of the smell
and taste, but I shall only tell you, that S. *Ambrose* the
glorious Bishop of *Milan* (who liv'd when the Church
kept Fasting days) calls him the *flowre fish,* or flowre
of fishes, and that he was so far in love with him, that
he would not let him pass without the honour of a
long Discourse; but I must; and pass on to tell you
how to take this dainty fish.

First, Note, That he grows not to the bigness of a
Trout; for the biggest of them do not usually exceed
eighteen inches, he lives in such Rivers as the Trout
does, and is usually taken with the same baits as the
Trout is, and after the same manner; for he will bite
both at the *Minnow,* or *Worm,* or *Fly,* (though he bites
not often at the Minnow) and is very gamesome at the
Fly, and much simpler, and therefore bolder than a
Trout; for he will rise twenty times at a fly, if you miss
him, and yet rise again. He has been taken with a fly
made of the red feathers of a *Parraketa,* a strange out-
landish bird, and he will rise at a fly not unlike a gnat

or a small moth, or indeed, at most flies that are not too big. He is a Fish that lurks close all winter, but is very pleasant and jolly after mid-*April,* and in *May,* and in the hot months: he is of a fine shape, his flesh is white, his teeth, those little ones that he has are in his throat, yet he has so tender a mouth, that he is oftner lost after an Angler has hooked him than any other Fish. Though there be many of these Fishes in *Trent,* and some other smaller rivers, as that which runs by *Salisbury,* yet he is not so general a Fish as the *Trout,* nor to me so good to eat or to Angle for. And so I shall take my leave of him, and come to some Observations of the *Salmon,* and how to catch him.

Observations of the Salmon, *with directions how to fish for him.*

Pisc. The *Salmon* is accounted the King of fresh-water-Fish, and is ever bred in Rivers relating to the Sea, yet so high or far from it as admits of no tincture of salt or brackishness; He is said to breed or cast his spawn in most Rivers in the month of *August:* some say, that then they dig a hole or grave in a safe place in the gravel, and there place their eggs or spawn (after the Melter his done his natural Office) and then hide it most cunningly, and cover it over with gravel and stones; and so leave it to their Creators protection, who by a gentle heat which he infuses into that cold element makes it brood and beget life in the spawn, and to become *Samlets* early in the spring next following.

The *Salmons* having spent their appointed time, and done this Natural Duty in the fresh waters, they then haste to the Sea before Winter, both the Melter and Spawner: but if they be stopt by *Flood-gates* or *Weres,* or lost in the fresh waters, then those so left behind, by degrees grow *sick,* and *lean,* and *unseasonable,* and *kipper,* that is to say, have bony gristles grow out of their lower chaps (not unlike a Hawks beak) which hinders their feeding, and in time such Fish so left behind, pine away and dye. 'Tis observed, that he may live thus one year from the Sea; but he then grows insipid and tasteless, and loses both his blood and strength, and pines and dies the second year. And 'tis noted, that those little *Salmons* called Skeggers, which abound in many Rivers relating to the *Sea,* are bred by such sick *Salmon,* that might not go to the Sea, and that though they abound, yet they never thrive to any considerable bigness.

But if the old *Salmon* gets to the Sea, then that gristle wears away, or is cast off (as the *Eagle* is said to cast his bill) and he recovers his strength, and comes next Summer to the same River (if it be possible) to enjoy the former pleasures that there possest him; for (as one has wittily observed) he has (like some persons of Honour and Riches, which have both their Winter and Summer houses) the fresh Rivers for Summer, and the salt water for Winter, to spend his life in; which is not (as Sir *Francis Bacon* hath observed in his *History of Life and Death*) above ten years: And it is to be observed, that though they grow big in the Sea, yet they grow not fat but in fresh Rivers; and it is observed, that the farther they get from the *Sea,* they be both the fatter and better.

Next, I shall tell you, that though they make very hard shift to get out of the fresh Rivers into the Sea, yet they will make harder shift to get out of the salt into the fresh Rivers, to spawn or possesse the pleasures that they have formerly found in them, to which end they will force themselves through *Flood-gates,* or over W*eires,* or *hedges,* or *stops* in the water, even beyond common belief. *Gesner* speaks of such places, as are known to be above eight foot high above water. And our *Cambden* mentions (in his *Brittannia*), the like wonder to be in *Pembroke-shire,* where the river T*ivy* falls into the Sea, and that the fall is so downright, and so high, that the people stand and wonder at the strength and slight that they see the *Salmon* use to get out of the Sea into the said River; and the manner and height of the place is so notable, that it is known far by the name of the *Salmon-leap;* concerning which, take this also out of *Michael Draiton,* my honest old friend.

And when the Salmon seeks a fresher stream to find,
(which hither from the Sea comes yearly by his kind)
As he towards season grows, and stems the watry tract
*W*here Tivy *falling down, makes an high cataract,*
Forc'd by the rising rocks that there her course oppose,
As though within her bounds they meant her to in-
    close;
Here when the labouring fish does at the foot arrive,
And finds that by his strength he does but vainly strive,
His tail takes in his mouth, and, bending like a bow
That's to ful compass drawn, aloft himself doth throw,
Then springing at his height as doth a little wand
That bended end to end, and started from mans hand,
Far off it self doth cast; so does the Salmon *vaut,*
And if at first he fail, his second Summer sought,

He instantly essaies, and, from his nimble ring,
Still yerking, never leaves until himself he fling
Above the opposing stream.——

And next I shall tell you, that it is observed by *Gesner* and others, that there is no better *Salmon* than in *England:* and that though some of our Northern Countries have as fat and as large as the River *Thames,* yet none are of so excellent a taste.

And as I have told you that Sir *Francis Bacon* observes, the age of a *Salmon* exceeds not ten years; so let me next tell you, that his growth is very sudden: it is said, that after he is got into the sea, he becomes from a *Samlet,* not so big as as Gudgion, to be a *Salmon,* in as short a time as a Gosling becomes to be a Goose. Much of this has been observed by tying a *Ribband* or some known *tape* or *thred,* in the tail of some young *Salmons,* which have been taken in Weirs as they have swimm'd toward the salt water, and then by taking a part of them again with the known mark at the same place at their return from the Sea, which is usually about six moneths after; and the like experiment hath been tryed upon young *Swallowes,* who have after six moneths absence, been observed to return to the same chimney, there to make their nests and habitations for the Summer following: which has inclined many to think, that every *Salmon* usually returns to the same River in which it was bred, as young *Pigeons* taken out of the same *Dove-cote,* have also been observed to do.

And you are yet to observe further, that the He *Salmon* is usually bigger than the Spawner, and that he is more kipper, and less able to endure a winter in the fresh water, than the She is, yet she is at that time of looking less kipper and better, as watry, and as bad meat.

And yet you are to observe, that as there is no general rule without an exception, so there are some few Rivers in this Nation, that have *Trouts* and *Salmon* in season in winter, as 'tis certain there be in the river W*y* in M*onmouth-shire,* where they be in season (as *Cambden* observes) from *September* till *April*. But my Scholar, the observation of this and many other things, I must in manners omit, because they will prove too large for our narrow compass of time, and therefore I shall next fall upon my direction how to fish for this *Salmon.*

And for that first, you shall observe, that usually he staies not long in a place (as *Trouts* wil) but (as I said) covets still to go nearer the Spring-head; and that he does not (as the *Trout* and many other fish) lie near the water side or bank or roots of trees, but swims in the deep and broad parts of the water, and usually in the middle, and near the ground; and that there you are to fish for him, and that he is to be caught as the *Trout* is, with a W*orm,* a M*innow* (which some call a P*enk*) or with a F*ly.*

And you are to observe, that he is very seldom observed to bite at a M*innow,* (yet sometimes he will) and not oft at a *fly,* but more usually at a W*orm,* and then most usually at a *Lob* or *Garden-worm,* which should be well scoured, that is to say, seven or eight daies in Moss before you fish with them: and if you double your time of eight into sixteen or more, into twenty or more daies, it is still the better, for the worms will still be clearer, tougher, and more lively, and continue so longer upon your hook, and they may be kept longer by keeping them cool and in fresh Moss.

Note also, that many use to Fish for a *Salmon* with a ring of wyre on the top of their Rod, through which the Line may run to as great a length as it is needful when he is hook'd. And to that end, some use a wheel about the middle of their Rod, or nearer their hand, which are to be observed either by seeing one of them, or a large demonstration of words.

And now I shall tell you, that which may be called a secret: I have been a fishing with old *Oliver Henly* (now with God), a noted Fisher, both for *Trout* and *Salmon,* and have observed, that he would usually take three or four worms out of his bag, and put them into a little box in his pocket, where he would usually let them continue half an hour or more, before he would bait his hook with them; I have asked him his reason, and he has replyed, He *did but pick the best out to be in a readinesse against he baited his hook the next time:* But he has been observed both by others, and my self, to catch more fish than I or any other body, that has ever gone a fishing with him could do, and especially *Salmons;* and I have been told lately by one of his most intimate and secret friends, that the box in which he put those worms, was anointed with a drop, or two, or three, of the Oil of *Ivy-berries,* made by expression or infusion, and that by the worms remaining in that box an hour, or a like time, they had incorporated a kind of smell that was irresistably attractive, enough to force any Fish within the smell of them, to bite. This I heard not long since from a friend, but have not tryed it; yet I grant it probable, and refer my Reader to Sir *Francis Bacons* Natural History, where he proves fishes may hear: and I am certain *Gesner* sayes, the *Otter* can smell in the water, and I know not but that Fish may do so too: 'tis left for a lover of Angling, or any that desires to improve that Art, to try this conclusion.

I shall also impart two other Experiments (but not tryed by my self) which I will deliver in the same words that they were given me (by an excellent Angler, and a very friend) in writing, he told me the latter was too good to be told, but in a learned language, lest it should be made common.

Take the stinking oil, drawn out of Polypody *of the* Oak *by a retort, mixt with* Turpentine, *and* Hive-honey, *and annoint your bait therewith, and it will doubtless draw the fish to it.*

The other is this: *Vulnera hederae grandissime inflectar sudant Balsamum oleo gelato, albicantique persimile, odoris vero longe suavissimi.*

'Tis supremely sweet to any fish, and yet *Asafoetida* may do the like.

But in these things I have no great faith, yet grant it

probable, and have had from some chimical men (namely, from Sir *George Hastings* and others) an affirmation of them to be very advantageous: but no more of these, especially not in this place.

I might here, before I take my leave of the *Salmon,* tell you, that there is more than one sort of them, as namely, a *Tecon,* and another called in some places a *Samlet,* or by some, a *Skegger:* but these (and others which I forbear to name) may be Fish of another kind (and differ, as we know a *Herring* and a *Pilcher* do), which I think are as different, as the Rivers in which they breed, and must by me be left to the disquisitions of men of more leisure, and of greater abilities, than I profess my self to have.

And lastly, I am to borrow so much of your promised patience, as to tell you that the *Trout* or *Salmon* being in season, have at their first taking out of the water (which continues during life) their bodies adorned, the one with such red spots, and the other with such black or blackish spots, which give them such an addition of natural beauty, as I think, was never given to any woman by the Artificial Paint or Patches in which they so much pride themselves in this Age. And so I shall leave them, and proceed to some Observations of the *Pike.*

Observations of the Luce *or* Pike, *with directions how to fish for him.*

Pisc. The mighty *Luce* or *Pike* is taken to be the Tyrant (as the *Salmon* is the King) of the fresh waters. 'Tis not to be doubted, but that they are bred, some by generation, and some not: as namely, of a Weed called *Pickerel-weed,* unless learned *Gesner* be much mistaken; for he sayes, this weed and other glutinous matter, with the help of the Suns heat in some particular Moneths, and some Ponds apted for it by nature, do become *Pikes.* But doubtless divers *Pikes* are bred after this manner, or are brought into some Ponds some other wayes that is past mans finding out, of which we have daily testimonies.

Sir *Francis Bacon* in his History of Life and Death, observes the *Pike* to be the longest lived of any freshwater-Fish, and yet he computes it to be not usually above forty years; and others think it to be not above ten years; and yet *Gesner* mentions a *Pike* taken in *Swedeland* in the year 1449. with a Ring about his neck, declaring he was put into the Pond by *Frederick* the second, more than two hundred years before he was last taken, as by the Inscription of that Ring (being Greek) was interpreted by the then Bishop of

Worms. But of this no more, but that it is observed, that the old or very great Pikes have in them more of state than goodness; the smaller or middle sized Pikes being by the most and choicest palates observed to be the best meat; and contrary, the Eele is observed to be the better for age and bigness.

All Pikes that live long prove chargeable to their Keepers, because their life is maintained by the death of so many other Fish, even those of his own kind, which has made him by some Writers to be called the *Tyrant* of the Rivers, or the *Fresh-water-woolf*, by reason of his bold, greedy devouring disposition; which is so keen, as *Gesner* relates, a man going to a Pond (where it seems a *Pike* had devoured all the fish) to water his Mule, had a *Pike* bit his Mule by the lips, to which the *Pike* hung so fast, that the Mule drew him out of the water, and by that accident the owner of the Mule got the *Pike*. And the same *Gesner* observes, that a Maid in *Poland* had a *pike* bit her by the foot as she was washing clothes in a Pond. And I have heard the like of a woman in *Killingworth* Pond, not far from *Coventry*. But I have been assured by my friend Mr. *Seagrave,* of whom I spake to you formerly, that keeps tame Otters, that he hath known a *pike* in extream hunger fight with one of his Otters for a Carp that the Otter had caught, and was then bringing out of the water. I have told you who relates these things, and tell you they are persons of credit, and shall conclude this observation, by telling you what a wise man has observed, *It is a hard thing to perswade the belly, because it has no ears.*

But if these relations be disbelieved, it is too evident to be doubted that a *pike* will devour a Fish of his own kind, that shall be bigger than his belly or throat will receive, and swallow a part of him, and let the other part remain in his mouth till the swallowed part be digested, and then swallow that other part that was in his mouth, and so put it over by degrees; which is not unlike the Oxe and some other beasts, taking their meat, not out of their mouth into their belly, but first into some place betwixt, and then chaw it, or digest it after, which is called *Chewing the cud*. And doubtless *pikes* will bite when they are not hungry, but as some think in very anger, when a tempting bait comes near to them.

And it is observed, that the *pike* will eat venomous things (as some kinds of *Frogs* are) and yet live without being harmed by them: for, as some say, he has in him a natural Balsom or Antidote against all poison: and others, that he never eats the venomous *Frog,* till he have first killed her, and then (as *Ducks* are observed to do to *Frogs* in Spawning time, at which time some *Frogs* are observed to be venomous) so throughly washt ner, by tumbling her up and down in the water, that he may devour her without danger. And *Gesner* affirms, that a *Polonian* Gentleman did faithfully assure him, he had seen two young Geese at one time in the belly of a *pike*. And doubtless a *pike* in his height of hunger will bite at and devour a dog that swimmes in a Pond, and there has been examples of it, or the like; for as I told you, *The belly has no ears when hunger comes upon it.*

The *pike* is also observed to be a solitary, melancholly and a bold Fish: Melancholly, because he alwayes swimmes or rests himself alone, and never swimmes in sholes or with company, as *R*oach and *D*ace, and most other Fish do: And bold, because he fears not a shadow, or to see or be seen of any body, as the *T*rout and *C*hub, and all other Fish do.

And it is observed by *Gesner,* that the Jaw-bones, and Hearts, and Galls of *pikes* are very medicinable for several diseases, or to stop blood, to abate Fevers, to cure Agues, to oppose or expel the infection of the Plague, and to be many wayes medicinable and useful for the good of Mankind; but he observes, that the biting of a *pike* is venomous and hard to be cured.

And it is observed, that the Pike is a fish that breeds but once a year, and that other fish (as namely *L*oaches) do breed oftner: as we are certain tame Pigeons do almost every month, and yet the Hawk a Bird of Prey (as the Pike is of Fish) breeds but once in twelve months: and you are to note, that his time of breeding or spawning is usually about the end of *February,* or, somewhat later, in *March,* as the weather proves colder or warmer; and to note, that his manner of breeding is thus, a He and a She Pike will usually go together out of a River into some ditch or creek, and that there the spawner casts her eggs, and the

Melter hovers over her all that time that she is casting her spawn, but touches her not.

I might say more of this, but it might be thought curiosity or worse, and shall therefore forbear it, and take up so much of your attention, as to tell you, that the best of Pikes are noted to be in *Rivers,* next those in great P*onds,* or M*eres,* and the worst in small Ponds.

But before I proceed further, I am to tell you that there is a great antipathy betwixt the Pike and some Frogs; and this may appear to the Reader of D*u-bravius* (a Bishop in B*ohemia*), who in his Book of Fish and Fish-ponds, relates what, he sayes, he saw with his own eyes, and could not forbear to tell the Reader. Which was:

As he and the B*ishop* Thurzo *were walking by a large Pond in* Bohemia, *they saw a Frog, when the Pike lay very sleepily and quiet by the shore side, leap upon his head, and the frog having exprest malice or anger by his swolne cheeks and staring eyes, did streatch out his legs and imbraced the* Pike*s head, and presently reached them to his eyes, tearing with them and his teeth those tender parts; the* Pike *moved with anguish, moves up and down the water, and rubs himself against weeds, and what ever he thought might quit him of his enemy; but all in vain, for the frog did continue to ride triumphantly, and to bite and torment the* Pike *till his strength failed, and then he sunk with the* Pike *to the bottome of the water; then presently the frog appeared again at the top and croaked, and semed to rejoyce like a Conqueror, and then presently* *retired to her secret hole. The Bishop, that had beheld the battel, called his fishermen to fetch his nets, and by all means to get the* Pike, *that they might declare what had hapned: and the* Pike *was drawn forth, and both his eyes eaten out, at which when they began to wonder, the Fisherman wished them to forbear, and assured them he was certain that* Pikes *were often so served.*

I told this (which is to be read in the sixth Chapter of the Book of *Dubravius*) unto a friend, who replied, It *was as improbable as to have the mouse scratch out the cats eyes.* But he did not consider, that there be fishing Frogs (which the *Dalmatians* call the Water-Devil) of which I might tell you as wonderful a story, but I shall tell you, that 'tis not to be doubted, but that there be some frogs so fearfull of the Water-snake, that, when they swim in a place in which they fear to meet with him, they get a reed acrosse into their mouthes, which if they two meet by accident, secures the frog from the strength and malice of the *Snake,* and note, that the frog swims the fastest.

And let me tell you, that as there be *Water* and *Land-frogs,* so there be *Land* and *Water-snakes.* Concerning which take this Observation, That the Land-snake breeds, and hatches her eggs, which become young Snakes in some old dunghill, or a like hot place; but the Water-snake, which is not venemous (and as I have been assured by a great observer of such secrets) does breed her young alive, which she does not then forsake, but bides with them, and in case of danger will take them all into her mouth and swim away from any apprehended danger, and then let them out again when she thinks all danger to be past: These be accidents that we Anglers sometimes see and often talk of.

But whither am I going? I had almost lost my self by remembring the Discourse of *Dubravius*. I will therefore stop here, and tell you according to my promise how to catch this fish.

His feeding is usually of *fish* or *frogs,* and sometimes a weed of his own, called *Pickrell-weed*. Of which I told you some think some Pikes are bred; for they have observed, that where none have been put into Ponds, yet they have there found many: and that there has been plenty of that weed in those Ponds, and that that weed both breeds and feeds them; but whether those Pikes so bred will ever breed by generation as the others do, I shall leave to the disquisitions of men of more curiosity and leasure than I professe my self to have; and shall proceed to tell you that you may fish for a Pike, either with a *ledger* or a *walking-bait*; and you are to note, that I call that a Ledger bait, which is fixed, or made to rest in one certain place when you shall be absent and I call that a walking bait, which you take with you, and have ever in motion. Concerning which two, I shall give you this direction, That your ledger bait is best to be a living bait, whether it be a fish or a frog; and that you may make them live the longer, you may or indeed you must take this course.

First, for your live bait of fish, a *Roach* or *Dace* is, (I think) best and most tempting, and a *Pearch* is the longest lived on a hook, and having cut off his fin on his back, which may be done without hurting him, you must take your knife (which cannot be too sharp), and betwixt the head and the fin on the back, cut or make an incision, or such a scar, as you may put the arming wier of your hook into it, with as little brusing or hurting the fish as art and dilligence will enable you to do, and so carrying your arming wier along his back, unto, or near the tail of your Fish, betwixt the skin and the body of it, draw out that wier or arming of your hook at another scar near to his tail: then tie him about it with thred, but no harder than of necessity you must to prevent hurting the fish; and the better to avoid hurting the fish, some have a kind of probe to open the way, for the more easie entrance and passage of your wier or arming: but as for these time, and a little experience will teach you better than I can by words; therefore I will for the present say no more of this, but come next to give you some directions, how to bait your hook with a frog.

VENA. But, good Master, did you not say even now, that some *Frogs* were venemous, and is it not dangerous to touch them?

PISC. Yes, but I will give you some Rules or Cautions concerning them: And first, you are to note, that there are two kinds of *Frogs;* that is to say (if I may so express my self), a *flesh,* and a *fish-frog*: by flesh *frogs,* I mean *frogs* that breed and live on the land; and of these there be several sorts also and colours, some being peckled, some greenish, some blackish, or brown: the green *Frog,* which is a small one, is, by *Topsel* taken to be venemous; and so is the *padock,* or *Frog-padog,* which usually keeps or breeds on the land, and is very large and bony, and big, especially the She frog of that kind; yet these will sometimes come into the water, but it is not often; and the land frogs are some of them observed by him, to breed by laying eggs; and others to breed of the slime and dust of the earth, and that in winter they turn to slime again, and that the next Summer that very slime returns to be a living creature; this is the opinion of *Pliny*: and *Cardanus*[1] undertakes to give a reason for the raining of Frogs: but if it were in my power, it should rain none but water-Frogs, for those, I think are not venemous, especially the right water-Frog, which about *February* or *March* breeds in ditches by slime, and blackish eggs in that slime: about which time of breeding the He and She Frogs are observed to use divers *Summer-sauts,* and to croak and make a noise, which the land-frog, or Padok frog never does. Now of these water-frogs, if you intend to fish with a frog for a Pike, you are to chuse the yellowest that you can get, for that the Pike ever likes best. And thus use your frog, that he may continue long alive.

Put your hook into his mouth, which you may easily do from the middle of *April* till *August,* and then the frogs mouth grows up, and he continues so for at least

[1] In his 16. Book, De *subtil. ex.*

six moneths without eating, but is sustained, none but he whose name is Wonderful, knowes how, I say, put your hook, I mean the arming wyer through his mouth, and out at his gills, and then with a fine needle and silk sow the upper part of his legg with onely one stitch to the arming wire of your hook, or tie the frogs leg above the upper joynt to the armed wire, and in so doing, use him as though you loved him, that is, harm him as little as you may possibly, that he may live the longer.

And now, having given you this direction for the baiting your ledger hook with a live Fish or frog, my next must be to tell you, how your hook thus baited must or may be used: and it is thus. Having fastned your hook to a line, which if it be not fourteen yards long, should not be lesse than twelve; you are to fasten that line to any bough near to a hole where a Pike is, or is likely to lie, or to have a haunt, and then wind your line on any forked stick, all your line except half a yard of it or rather more, and split that forked stick with such a nick or notch at one end of it, as may keep the line from any more of it ravelling from about the stick, then so much of it as you intended; and chuse your forked stick to be of that bigness as may keep the fish or frog from pulling the forked stick under the water till the Pike bites, and then the Pike having pulled the line forth of the clift or nick of that stick in which it was gently fastned, will have line enough to go to his hold and powch the bait: and if you would have this ledger bait to keep at a fixt place, undisturbed by wind or other accidents which may drive it to the shore side (for you are to note, that it is likeliest to catch a Pike in the midst of the water), than hang a small Plummet of lead, a stone, or piece of tyle, or a turf in a string, and cast it into the water, with the forked stick, to hang upon the ground to be an Anchor to keep the forked stick from moving out of your intended place till the Pike come. This I take to be a very good way, to use so many ledger baits as you intend to make trial of.

Or if you bait your hooks thus with live Fish or Frogs, and in a windy day, fasten them thus to a bough or bundle of straw, and by the help of that wind can get them to move crosse a *pond* or *mere,* you are like to stand still on the shore and see sport, if there be any store of *Pikes,* or these live Baits may make sport, being tied about the body or wings of a *Goose* or *Duck,* and she chased over a *Pond*: and the like may be done with turning three or four live baits thus fastened to bladders, or boughs, or bottles of hay or flags, to swim down a River, whilst you walk quietly alone on the shore, and are still in expectation of sport. The rest must be taught you by practice; for time will not allow me to say more of this kind of fishing with live baits.

And for your dead bait for a *Pike,* for that you may be taught by one dayes going a fishing with me, or any other body that fishes for him, for the baiting your hook with a dead *Gudgeon* or a *Roach,* and moving it up and down the Water, is too easie a thing to take up any time to direct you to do it; and yet, because I cut you short in that, I will commute for it, by telling you that that was told me for a secret: it is this,

Dissolve Gum *of* Ivy *in* Oyle *of* Spike, *and therewith annoynt your dead bait for a* Pike, *and then cast it into a likely place, and when it has lain a short time at the bottom, draw it towards the top of the water and so up the stream, and it is more then likely that you have a* Pike *follow with more than common eagerness.*

And some affirm, that any bait annointed with the marrow of the Thigh-bone of an **H***ern* is a great temptation to any Fish.

These have not been tried by me, but told me by a friend of note, that pretended to do me a courtesie, but if this direction to catch a *pike* thus do you no good, yet I am certain this direction how to roast him when he is caught, is choicely good, for I have tryed it; and it is somewhat the better for not being common: but with my direction you must take this Caution, that your *pike* must not be a smal one, that is, it must be more than half a Yard, and should be bigger.

First, open your Pike *at the gills, and if need be, cut also a little slit towards his belly; out of these take his guts, and keep his liver, which you are to shred very small with* Time, Sweet-margerome *and a little* Winter-savoury; *to these put some pickled* Oysters, *and some* Anchovies *two or three, both these last whole (for the* Anchovies *will melt, and the* Oysters *should not); to these you must adde also a pound of sweet butter, which you are to mix with the herbs that are* shred, and let them all be well salted (if the Pike be more than a yard long, then you may put into these herbs more than a pound, or if he be lesse, then lesse Butter will suffice): these being thus mixt with a blade or two of Mace, must be put into the Pikes belly, and then his belly sowed up, and so sowed up, as to keep all the Butter in his belly if it be possible, if not, then as much of it as you possible can, but take not off the scales; then you are to thrust the spit through his mouth out at his tayl, and then with four, or five, or six split sticks, or very thin lathes, and a convenient quantity of Tape or Filliting, these lathes are to be tyed round about the Pikes body from his head to his tayl, and the Tape tyed somewhat thick to prevent his breaking or falling off from the spit, let him be roasted very leasurely, and often basted with Claret wine, and Anchovyes, and Butter mixt together, and also with what moisture falls from him into the pan: when you have roasted him sufficiently you are to hold under him (when you unwind or cut the Tape that tyes him) such a dish as you purpose to eat him out of; and let him fall into it with the sawce that is rosted in his belly, and by this means the Pike will be kept unbroken and compleat: then to the sawce, which was within, and also in the pan, you are to adde a fit quantity of the best Butter, and to squeeze the juyce of three or four Oranges: lastly, you may either put into the Pike with the Oysters, two cloves of Garlick, and take it whole out, when the Pike is cut off the spit, or to give the *sawce a* hogo, *let the dish (into which you let the Pike fall) be rubbed with it: the using or not using of this Garlick is left to your discretion.*   M. B.

This dish of meat is too good for any but Anglers or honest men: and I trust, you will prove both, and therefore I have trusted you with this secret.

Let me next tell you, that *Gesner* tells us there are no Pikes in *Spain,* and that the largest are in the Lake *Thrasimane* in *Italy*; and the next, if not equall to them, are the Pikes of *England,* and that in *England, Lincoln* shire boasteth to have the biggest. Just so doth *Sussex* boast of four sorts of fish; namely an *Arundell Mullet,* a *Chichester Lobster,* a *Chelsey Cockle,* and an *Amerly Trout.*

But I will take up no more of your time with this relation, but proceed to give you some observations of the *Carp,* and how to angle for him.

Observations of the Carp, *with Directions how to fish for him.*

Pisc. The Carp is the Queen of Rivers, a stately, a good, and a very subtil fish, that was not at first bred, nor hath been long in *England*, but is now naturalized. It is said, they were brought hither by one Mr. *Mascal* a Gentleman that then lived at *Plumsted* in *Sussex,* a County that abounds more with this fish than any in this Nation.

You may remember that I told you, *Gesner* says, there are no *Pikes* of *Spain*; and doubtless, there was a time, about a hundred or a few more years ago, when there were no *Carps* in *England,* as may seem to be affirmed by S. *Richard Baker,* in whose Chronicle you may find these Verses.

> *Hops and Turkies, Carps and Beer*
> *Came into* England *all in a year.*

And doubtless as of Sea-fish the *Herring* dies soonest out of the water, and of fresh-water-fish the *Trout,* so (except the *Eele*) the *Carp* indures most hardness, and lives longest out of his own proper Element. And therefore the report of the Carps being brought out of a forraigne into this Nation is the more probable.

Carps and Loaches are observed to Breed several months in one year, which Pikes and most other Fish do not. And this is partly proved by tame and wild *Rabbits,* as also by some *Ducks,* which will lay egs nine of the twelve moneths, and yet there be other *Ducks* that lay not longer then about one month. And it is the rather believed, because you shall scarce or never take a *Male Carp* without a *Melt,* or a *Female* without a *Roe* or *spawn,* and for the most part very much; and especially all the Summer Season; and it is observed, that they breed more naturally in ponds then in running waters (if they breed there at all); and that those that live in Rivers are taken by men of the best palats to be much the better meat.

And it is observed, that in some ponds *Carps* will not breed, especially in cold ponds; but where they will breed, they breed innumerably; *Aristotle* and *Pliny* say, six times in a year, if there be no *Pikes* nor *Pearch* to devour their Spawn, when it is cast upon grasse, or flags or weeds, where it lies ten or twelve dayes before it be enlivened.

The *Carp,* if he have water-room and good feed, will grow to a very great bignesse and length: I have heard, to be much above a yard long. 'Tis said (by *Jovius,* who hath writ of Fishes) that in the Lake *Lurian* in *Italy, Carps* have thriven to be more then fifty pound weight, which is the more probable, for as the *Bear* is conceiv'd and born suddenly; and being born is but short-liv'd: So on the contrary, the *Elephant* is said to be two years in his dams belly (some think he is ten years in it) and being born growes in bignesse twenty years; and 'tis observ'd too that he lives to the Age of a hundred years. And 'tis also observ'd that the *Crocadile* is very long-liv'd, and more then that, that all that long life he thrives in bignesse, and so I think some *Carps* do, especially in some places; though I never saw one above 23. inches, which was a great and a goodly Fish: But have been assured there are of a far greater size, and in *England* too.

Now, as the increase of *Carps* is wonderful for their number; so there is not a reason found out, I think by any, why they should breed in some ponds, and not in others of the same nature, for soil and all other circumstances: and as their breeding, so are their decayes also very mysterious: I have both read it, and been told by a Gentleman of tryed honesty, that he has known sixty or more large *Carps* put into several ponds near to a house, where by reason of the stakes in the ponds, and the Owners constant being near to them, it was impossible they should be stole away from him: and that when he has after three or four years emptyed the pond, and expected an increase from them by breeding young ones (for that they might do so he had, as the rule is, put in three Melters for one Spawner) he has, I say, after three or four years, found neither a young nor old *Carp* remaining. And the like I have known of one that has almost watched the pond, and at a like distance of time, at the fishing of a pond, found of seventy or eighty large *Carps* not above five or six: and that he had forborn longer to fish the said pond, but that he saw in a hot day in Summer, a large *Carp* swim near to the top of the water with a Frog upon his head, and that he upon that occasion caused his pond to be let dry: and I say, of seventy or eighty *Carps,* only found five or six in the said pond, and those very sick and lean, and with every one a Frog sticking so fast on the head of the said *Carps,* that the Frog would not be got off without extreme force or killing: and the Gentleman that did affirm this to me, told me he saw it, and did declare his belief to be (and I also believe the same) that he thought the other *Carps* that were so strangely lost, were so killed by frogs, and then devoured.

But I am faln into this Discourse by accident, of which I might say more, but it has proved longer than I intended, and possibly may not to you be considerable; I shall therefore give you three or four more short observations of the *Carp,* and then fall upon some directions how you shall fish for him.

The age of *Carps* is by Sir *Francis Bacon* (in his History of Life and Death) observed to be but ten years; yet others think they live longer. *Gesner* saies a *Carp* has been known to live in the *Palatinate* above a hundred years: But most conclude, that (contrary to the *Pike* or *Luce*) all *Carps* are the better for age and bigness, the tongues of *Carps* are noted to be choice and costly meat, especially to them that buy them: but *Gesner* saies, *Carps* have no tongue like other Fish, but a piece of flesh like Fish in their mouth like to a tongue, and should be called a palate: But it is certain it is choicely good, and that the *Carp* is to be reckoned amongst those leather-mouthed fish, which I told you have their teeth in their throat, and for that reason he is very seldom lost by breaking his hold, if your hook be once stuck into his chaps.

I told you, that Sir *Francis Bacon* thinks that the *Carp* lives but ten years, but *Janus Dubravius* has writ a Book of Fish and Fish-ponds, in which he saies, That *Carps* begin to Spawn at the age of three years, and continue to do so till thirty: he saies also, That in the time of their breeding, which is in Summer, when the Sun hath warmed both the earth and water, and so apted them also for generation, that then three or four Male-*Carps* will follow a Female, and that then she putting on a seeming coyness, they force her through weeds and flags, where she lets fall her Eggs or Spawn, which sticks fast to the weeds, and then they let fall their Melt upon it, and so it becomes in a short time to be a living fish; and as I told you, it is thought the *Carp* does this several moneths in the year, and most believe that most fish breed after this manner, except the Eele: and it has been observed, that when the Spawner has weakened her self by doing that natural office, that two or three Melters have helped her from off the weeds, by bearing her up on both sides, and guarding her into the deep. And you may note, that though this may seem a curiosity not worth observing, yet others have judged it worth their time and costs to make *Glasse-hives,* and order them in such a manner as to see how *Bees* have bred and made their *Honey-*

combs, and how they have obeyed their King, and governed their Common-wealth. But it is thought that all *Carps* are not bred by generation, but that some breed other wayes, as some *Pikes* do.

The Physicians make the *galls* and *stones* in the heads of *Carps* to be very medicinable; but 'tis not to be doubted but that in *Italy* they make great profit of the Spawn of *Carps,* by selling it to the *Jewes,* who make it into red *Caviare,* the *Jewes* not being by their Law admitted to eat of *Caviare* made of the *Sturgion,* that being a Fish that wants scales, and (as may appear in *Levit.* 11.) by them to be reputed unclean.

Much more might be said out of him, and out of *Aristotle,* which *Dubravius* often quotes in his Discourse of Fishes; but it might rather perplex than satisfie you, and therefore I shall rather chuse to direct you how to catch, than spend more time in discoursing either of the nature or the breeding of this *Carp,* or of any more circumstances concerning him, but yet I shall remember you of what I told you before, that he is a very subtil Fish, and hard to be caught.

And my first direction is, that if you will Fish for a *Carp,* you must put on a very large measure of *patience*; especially to fish for a *River Carp*: I have known a very good Fisher angle diligently four or six hours in a day, for three or four daies together for a *River Carp,* and not have a bite: and you are to note, that in some ponds it is as hard to catch a Carp as in a River; that is to say, where they have store of feed, and the water is of a clayish colour: But you are to remember, that I have told you there is no rule without an exception, and therefore being possest with that hope and patience which I wish to all Fishers, especially to the *Carp-Angler,* I shall tell you with what bait to fish for him. But first you are to know, that it must be either early or late; and let me tell you, that in hot weather (for he will seldom bite in cold) you cannot be too early or too late at it. And some have been so curious as to say, the 10. of *April* is a fatal day for Carps.

The Carp bites either at worms or at paste, and of worms I think the blewish Marsh or Meadow worm is best, but possibly another worm not too big may do as well, and so may a green Gentle; And as for pastes, there are almost as many sorts as there are Medicines for the Toothach, but doubtless sweet pastes are best; I mean, pastes made with honey or with sugar: which, that you may the better beguile this crafty Fish, should be thrown into the Pond or place in which you fish for him some hours before you undertake your tryal of skill with the Angle-rod: and doubtless if it be thrown into the water a day or two before, at severall times and in small pellets, you are the likelier when you fish for the Carp to obtain your desired sport: or in a large Pond to draw them to any certain place, that they may the better and with more hope be fished for, you are to throw into it in some certain place, either Grains or Bloud mixt with Cow-dung, or with Bran; or any Garbage, as Chickens guts or the like, and then some of your small sweet pellets with which you purpose to angle: and these small pellets being a few of them also thrown in as you are Angling.

And your paste must be thus made: Take the flesh of a Rabbet or Cat cut small, and Bean-flowre, and if that may not be easily got, get other flowre, and then mix these together, and put to them either Sugar, or Honey, which I think better, and then beat these together in a Mortar, or sometimes work them in your hands (your hands being very clean) and then make it into a Ball, or two, or three, as you like best for your use: but you must work or pound it so long in the Mortar, as to make it so tough as to hang upon your hook without washing from it, yet not too hard: or that you may the better keep it on your hook, you may knead with your paste a little (and not much) white or yellowish wool.

And if you would have this paste keep all the year for any other Fish, then mix with it *Virgins wax* and *clarified honey,* and work them together with your hands before the Fire, then make these in to balls, and they will keep all the year.

And if you fish for a Carp with Gentles, then put upon your hook a small piece of Scarlet about this big-ness ☐, it being soked in, or anointed with *Oyl of Peter,* called by some *Oyl of the Rock,* and if your Gentles be put two or three dayes before into a box or horn anointed with honey, and so put upon your hook, as to preserve them to be living, you are as like to kill this crafty fish this way as any other: But still as you are fishing chaw a little white or brown bread in your mouth, and cast it into the pond about the place where your Flote swims. Other baites there be, but these with diligence, and patient watchfulness, will do it better than any that I have ever practised, or heard of: And yet I shall tell you, that the crumbs of white bread and honey made into a paste is a good bait for a *Carp,* and you know it is more easily made. And having said thus much of the *Carp,* my next discourse shall be of the *Bream,* which shall not prove so tedious, and therefore I desire the continuance of your attention.

But first I will tell you how to make this *Carp* that is so curious to be caught, so curious a dish of meat as shall make him worth all your labour; and though it is not without some trouble and charges, yet it will recompence both.

Take a Carp *(alive if possible), scour him, and rub him clean with water and salt, but scale him not, then open him, and put him with his bloud and his liver (which you must save when you open him) into a small pot or kettle; then take sweet* Margerome, Time *and* Parsley, *of each half a handful, a sprig of Rosemary, and another of Savoury, bind them into two or three small bundles, and put them to your* Carp, *with four or five whole* Onyons, *twenty pickled* Oysters, *and three* Anchovies. *Then pour upon your* Carp *as much claret wine as will onely cover him; and season your claret well with salt,* Cloves *and* Mace, *and the rinds of* Oranges *and* Lemmons, *cover your pot and set it on a quick fire, till it be sufficiently boiled; then take out the* Carp *and lay it with the broth into the dish, and pour upon it a quarter of a pound of fresh butter melted and beaten, with half a dozen spoonfuls of the broth, the yolks of two or three eggs, and some of the herbs shred, garnish your dish with Lemmons and so serve it up.* Dr. T.

Observations of the Bream, and directions to catch him.

PISC. The Bream being at a full growth is a large and stately Fish; he will breed both in Rivers and ponds: but loves best to live in ponds, and where, if he likes the water and Air, he will grow not only to be very large, but as fat as a Hog: he is by *Gesner* taken to be more pleasant or sweet then wholsome; this Fish is long in growing, but breeds exceedingly in a water that pleases him, yea, in many Ponds so fast, as to over-store them, and starve the other Fish.

He is very broad with a forked tail, and his scales set in excellent order, he hath large eyes and a narrow sucking mouth; he hath two sets of teeth, and a lozing like bone, a bone to help his grinding. The Melter is observed to have two large Melts, and the Female two large bags of eggs or spawn.

Gesner reports, that in *Poland* a certain and a great number of large Breames were put into a Pond, which in the next following winter was frozen up into one intire ice, and not one drop of water remaining, nor one of these fish to be found, though they were dili-gently searcht for; and yet the next Spring when the ice was thawed, and the weather warm, they all appeared again. This *Gesner* affirms, and I quote my Author, because it seems almost as incredible as the *Resurrection* to an *Athiest*. But it may win something in point of believing it, to him that considers the breeding or renovation of the Silk-worm, and of many insects. And that is considerable which Sir *Francis Bacon* observes in his History of Life and Death (*fol.* 20.) that there be some herbs that die and spring every year, and some endure longer.

But though some do not, yet the *French* esteem this Fish highly, and to that end have this Proverb, **He that hath Breams in his pond is able to bid his friend welcome.** And it is noted, that the best part of a Breame is his belly and head.

Some say, that *Breams* and *Roaches* will mix their eggs, and melt together, and so there is in many places a Bastard breed of Breams, that never come to be either large or good, but very numerous.

The Baits good to catch this *Bream* are many. First, paste made of brown bread and honey, gentles, or the brood of wasps that be young, and then not unlike Gentles; and should be hardned in an oven, or dried on a tile before the fire; or there is at the root of docks, or flags, or rushes in watry places, a worm not unlike a Magot, at which Tench will bite freely. Or he will bite at a Grashopper with his legs nipt off in *June* and *July,* or at several flies under water, which may be found on flags that grow near to the water side. I doubt not but that there be many other baits that are good, but I will turn them all into this most excellent one, either for a *Carp* or *Bream,* in any river or Mere: it was given to me by a most honest and excellent Angler, and hoping you will prove both, I will impart it to you.

1. Let your bait be as big a red worm as you can find, without a knot. Get a pint or quart of them in an evening in garden walks, or chalky Commons after a showre of rain; and put them with clean Mosse well washed and picked, and the water squeezed out of the Moss as dry as you can, into an earthen pot or pipkin set dry, and change the Moss fresh every three or four dayes for three weeks or a moneth together, then your bait will be at the best.

2. Having thus prepared your baits, get your tackling ready and fitted after this sort. Take three long Angling Rods, and as many and more silk, or silk and hair lines, and as many large Swan or Goose-quil floats. Then take a piece of Lead made after this manner, and fasten them to the lower ends of your Lines. Then fasten your link-hook also to the lead, and to the end of your Line, let there be about a foot or ten inches between the lead and the hook, but be sure the lead be heavy enough to sink the float or quil under water, and not the quil to bear up the Lead. Note, that your link next the hook may be smaller than the rest of your line, if you dare adventure for fear of taking the *Pike* or *Pearch,* who will assuredly visit your hooks, till they be taken out

(as I will shew you afterwards) before either *Carp* or *Bream* will come near to bite. Note also, that when the worm is well baited, it will crawl up and down, as far as the Lead will give leave, which much inticeth the Fish to bite without suspicion.

3. Having thus prepared your baits, and fitted your tackling, repair to the River, where you have seen them to swim in skuls or shoals in the Summer time in a hot afternoon, about three or four of the clock, and watch their going forth of their deep holes and returning (which you may well discern) for they return about four of the clock most of them seeking food at the bottom, yet one or two will lie on the top of the water, rolling and tumbling themselves, whilst the rest are under him at the bottom, and so you shall perceive him to keep Sentinel: then mark where he playes most, and stayes longest (which commonly is in the broadest and deepest place of the River), and there, or near thereabouts, at a clear bottom, and a convenient landing place, take one of your Angles ready fitted as aforesaid, and sound the bottom, about eight or ten foot deep, two yards from the bank is the best. Then consider with your self, whether that water will rise or fall by the next morning by reason of any water-mills near, and according to your discretion take the depth of the place, where you mean after to cast your ground-bait, and to fish, to half an inch; that the Lead lying on or near the ground-bait, the top of the float may only appear upright half an inch above the water.

Thus you having found and fitted for the place and depth thereof, then go home and prepare your ground-bait, which is next to the fruit of your labours to be regarded.

The Ground-Bait.

You shall take a peck, or a peck and a half (according to the greatness of the stream, and deepness of the water, where you mean to angle) of sweet gross-ground barely-malt, and boil it in a kettle (one or two warms is enough) then strain it through a Bag into a tub (the liquor whereof hath often done my Horse much good) and when the bag and malt is near cold, take it down to the water-side about eight or nine of the clock in the evening, and not before; cast in two parts of your ground-bait, squeezed hard between both your hands, it will sink presently to the bottom, and be sure it may rest in the very place where you mean to angle; if the stream run hard or move a little, cast your malt in handfuls the higher upwards the stream. You may between your hands close the Malt so fast in handfuls, that the water will hardly part it with the fall.

Your ground thus baited, and tackling fitted, leave your bag with the rest of your tackling, and ground-bait near the sporting-place all night, and in the morning about three or four of the clock visit the water-side (but not too near) for they have a Watch-man, and are watchful themselves.

Then gently take one of your three rods, and bait

your hook, casting it over your ground-bait, and gently and secretly draw it to you till the Lead rests about the middle of the ground-bait.

Then take a second Rod and cast in about a yard above, and your third a yard below the first Rod, and stay the Rods in the ground, but go your self so far from the water-side, that you perceive nothing but the top of the floats, which you must watch most diligently, then when you have a bite, you shall perceive the top of your float to sink suddenly into the water; yet nevertheless be not too hasty to run to your Rods, until you see that Line goes clear away; then creep to the water-side, and give as much Line as possibly you can: if it be a *Carp* or *Bream,* they will go to the farther side of the River, then strike gently, and hold your Rod at a bent a little while; for if you both pull, you are sure to lose your Game, for either your line or hook, or hold will break; and after you have overcome them, they will make noble sport, and are very shie to be landed. The *Carp* is far stronger and mettlesome than the *Bream.*

Much more is to be observed in this kind of Fish and Fishing, but it is far fitter for experience and discourse than paper. Only thus much is necessary for you to know, and to be mindful and careful of, That if the *Pike* or Pearch do breed in that River, they will be sure to bite first, and must first be taken. And for the most part they are very large, and will repair to your ground-bait, not that they will eat of it, but will feed and sport themselves amongst the young Fry, that gather about and hover over the Bait.

The way to discern the *Pike* and to take him, if you mistrust your *Bream* hook, (for I have taken a *Pike* a yard long several times at my *Bream*-hooks, and sometimes he hath had the luck to share my line.)

Take a small B*leak,* or R*oach,* or Gu*dgion,* and bait it, and set it alive among your Rods two foot deep from the Cork, with a little red worm on the point of the hook, then take a few crums of White-bread, or some of the ground-bait, and sprinkle it gently amongst your Rods. If Mr. P*ike* be there, then the little Fish will skip out of the water, but the live-set Bait is sure to be taken.

Thus continue your sport from four in the morning till eight, and if it be a gloomy windy day, they will bite all day long. But this is too long to stand to your rods at one place, and it will spoil your evening sport that day, which is this,

About four of the clock in the Afternoon repair to your baited place, and as soon as you come to the water side, cast in one half of the rest of your ground-bait, and stand off: then whilst the Fish are gathering together (for there they will most certainly come for their supper), you may take a pipe of Tobacco; and then in with your three rods as in the morning: You will find excellent sport that evening till eight of the clock; then cast in the residue of your ground-bait, and next morning by four of the clock visit them again for four hours, which is the best sport of all; and after that let them rest till you and your friends have a mind to more sport.

From St. *James* Tide until *Bartholomew* Tide is the best, when they have had all the Summers food, they are the fattest.

Observe lastly, That after three or four dayes fishing together, your Game will be very shie and wary; and you shall hardly get above a bite or two at a baiting: then your onely way is to desist from your sport about two or three dayes; and in the mean time (on the place you late baited, and again intend to bait) you shall take a turf of green, but short grass, as big or bigger than a round Trencher; to the top of this turf, on the green side, you shall with a Needle and green thred fasten one by one as many little red worms as will near cover all the turf; Then take a round board or Trencher, make a hole in the middle thereof, and through the turf placed on the board or Trencher, with a string or cord as long as is fitting, tied to a pole, let it down to the bottom of the water for the Fish to feed upon without disturbance about two or three dayes; and after that you have drawn it away, you may fall to, and enjoy your former recreation.   B. A.

Observations of the Tench, *and advice how to angle for him.*

Pisc. The T*ench,* the Physician of Fishes, is observed to love Ponds better than Rivers, and to love pits better than either; yet *Cambden* observes there is a R*iver* in D*orset-shire* that abounds with Tenches, but doubtless they retire to the most deep and quiet places in it.

This fish hath very large Fins, very small and smooth Scales, a red circle about his Eyes, which are big and of a gold colour, and that from either Angle of his mouth there hangs down a little Barb; in every T*enches* head there are two little stones, which forraign Physitians make great use of, but he is not commended for wholesome meat, though there be very much use made of them, for outward applications. *Randeletius* sayes. That at his being at R*ome, he saw a great cure done by applying a* T*ench to the feet of a very sick man.* This he says was done after an unusual manner by certain Jews. And it is observed, that many of those people have many secrets, yet unknown to Christians; secrets that have never yet been written, but have been since the dayes of their *Solomon* (who knew the nature of all things, even from the Cedar to the Shrub) delivered by tradition from the Father to the Son, and so from generation to generation without writing, or (unlesse it was casually) without the least communicating them to any other Nation or Tribe: for to do that they accounted a profanation. And yet it is thought that they, or some Spirit worse than they, first told us, that Lice swallowed alive were a certain cure for the Yellow-Jaundice. This and other medicines were discover'd by them or by revelation, for doubtless we attain'd them not by study.

Well, this fish, besides his eating, is very usefull both dead and alive for the good of mankind. But, I will meddle no more with that; my honest humble Art teaches no such boldnesse; there are too many foolish medlers in Physick and Divinity, that think themselves fit to meddle with hidden secrets, and so bring destruction to their followers. I'le not meddle with them farther than to wish them wiser; and shall tell you next (for, I hope, I may be so bold) that the Tench is the Physitian of fishes, to the Pike especially, and that the Pike, being either sick or hurt, is cured by the touch of the Tench. And it is observed, that the Tyrant Pike will not be a Wolf to his Physitian, but forbears to devour him though he be never so hungry.

This fish that carries a natural Balsome in him to cure both himself and others, loves yet to feed in very foul water, and amongst weeds. And yet I am sure he eats pleasantly, and, doubtlesse, you will think so too if you taste him. And I shall therefore proceed to give you some few, and but a few directions how to catch this Tench, of which I have given you these observations.

He will bite at a Paste made of brown bread and honey, or at a Marsh-worm, or a Lob-worm, he inclines very much to any paste with which Tar is mixt, and he will bite also at a smaller worm, with his head nipp'd off, and a Cod-worm put on the hook before that worm; and I doubt not but that he will also in the three hot months (for in the nine colder he stirs not much) bite at a Flag-worm, or at a green Gentle, but can positively say no more of the Tench, he being a Fish that I have not often Angled for; but I wish my honest Scholar may, and be ever fortunate when he fishes.

CHAPTER XII

Observations of the Pearch, *and directions how to fish for him.*

Pisc. The P*earch* is a very good, and a very bold biting fish; He is one of the Fishes of prey, that like the P*ike* and T*rout,* carries his teeth in his mouth which is very large, and he dare venture to kill and devour several other kinds of fish: he has a hook't or hog back, which is armed with sharp and stiffe bristles, and all his skin armed or covered over with thick, dry, hard scales, and hath (which few other Fish have) two Fins on his back. He is so bold, that he will invade one of his own kind, which the Pike will not do willingly, and you may therefore easily believe him to be a bold biter.

The P*earch* is of great esteem in *Italy* saith *Aldrovandus,* and especially the least are there esteemed a daintie dish. And G*esner* prefers the P*earch* and P*ike* above the T*rout,* or any fresh-water-Fish: he sayes the G*ermanes* have this Proverb, *More wholsom than a* P*earch of* R*hine*: and he sayes the River-P*earch* is so wholsome, that Physicians allow him to be eaten by wounded men or men in Feavers, or to Women in Child-bed.

He spawns but once a year, and is by Physicians held

196

very nutritive: yet by many to be hard of digestion: They abound more in the River *Poe* and in *England* (sayes *Randeletius*) then other parts, and have in their brain a stone, which is in forraign parts sold by Apothecaries, being there noted to be very medicinable against the stone in the reins: These be a part of the commendations which some Phylosophical brains have bestowed upon the fresh-water *Pearch*: yet they commend the Sea-*Pearch,* which is known by having but one fin on his back, (of which they say, we *English* see but a few) to be a much better fish.

The *Pearch* grows slowly, yet will grow, as I have been credibly informed, to be almost two foot long; for my informer told me, such a one was not long since taken by Sir *Abraham Williams,* a Gentleman of worth, and a lover of Angling, that yet lives, and I wish he may: this was a deep bodied Fish: and doubtless durst have devoured a *Pike* of half his own length: for I have told you, he is a bold Fish, such a one as but for extreme hunger, the *Pike* will not devour; for to affright the *Pike* and save himself, the *Pearch* will set up his fins, much like as a *Turkie-Cock* will sometimes set up his tail.

But, my Scholar, the Pearch is not only valiant to defend himself, but he is (as I said) a bold biting fish, yet he will not bite at all seasons of the year; he is very abstemious in Winter, yet will bite then in the midst of the day if it be warm: and note that all Fish bite best about the midst of a warm day in Winter, and he hath been observed by some, not usually to bite till the

Mulberry-tree buds, that is to say, till extreme frosts be past that Spring; for when the *Mulberry-tree* blossomes, many Gardners observe their forward fruit to be past the danger of Frosts, and some have made the like observation of the *Pearches* biting.

But bite the Pearch will, and that very boldly: and as one has wittily observed, if there be twenty or forty in a hole, they may be at one standing all catch'd one after another; they being, as he saies, like the wicked of the world, not afraid though their fellows and companions perish in their sight. And you may observe, that they are not like the solitary Pike, but love to accompany one another, and march together in troops.

And the baits for this bold Fish are not many; I mean, he will bite as well at some, or at any of these three, as at any or all others whatsoever: a *Worm,* a *Minnow,* or a little *Frog* (of which you may find many in hay-time), and of *worms,* the Dunghil-worm called a *Brandling,* I take to be best, being well scowred in Moss or Fennel; or at a worm that lies under a cow-turd with a blewish head. And if you *rove* for a Pearch with a *Minnow,* then it is best to be alive: you sticking your hook through his back-fin, or a *Minnow* with the hook in his upper lip, and letting him swim up and down about mid-water, or a little lower, and you still keeping him to about that depth, by a Cork, which ought not to be a very little one: and the like way you are to Fish for the Pearch, with a small frog, your hook being fastned through the skin of his leg, towards the upper part of it: And lastly, I

will give you but this advice, that you give the Pearch
time enough when he bites, for there was scarce ever
any Angler that has given him too much. And now I
think best to rest my self, for I have almost spent my
spirits with talking so long.

VENA. Nay, good Master, one fish more, for you see
it rains still, and you know our Angles are like mony
put to usurie; they may thrive, though we sit still and
do nothing, but talk and enjoy one another. Come,
come the other fish, good Master.

PISC. But Scholar, have you nothing to mixe with
this discourse, which now grows both tedious and tire-
some? shall I have nothing from you that seems to
have both a good memorie, and a chearful Spirit?

VENA. Yes, Master, I will speak you a Copy of Verses
that were made by Doctor *Donne,* and made to shew
the world that he could make soft and smooth Verses
when he thought smoothness worth his labour; and I
love them the better, because they allude to Rivers, and
fish and fishing. They be these:

> *Come live with me, and by my* Love,
> *And we will some new pleasures prove,*
> *Of golden sands, and Christal brooks,*
> *With silken lines, and silver hooks.*

> *There will the* River *whispering run,*
> *Warm'd by thy eyes more than the* Sun;
> *And there th' inamel'd fish will stay,*
> *Begging themselves they may betray.*

When thou wilt swim in that live bath,
Each fish, which every channel hath,
Most amorously to thee will swim,
Gladder to catch thee, then thou him.

If thou, to be so seen, beest loath
By Sun or Moon, thou darknest both,
And if mine eyes have leave to see,
I need not their light, having thee.

Let others freeze with Angling reeds,
And cutt their legs with shels and weeds,
Or treacherously poor fish beset
With strangling snares or windowy net.

Let course bold hands, from slimy nest,
The bedded fish in banks outwrest,
Let curious Traytors sleave silk flies,
To 'witch poor wandring fishes eyes.

For thee, thou needs no such deceit,
For thou thy self art thine own bait:
That fish that is not catcht thereby,
Is wiser far, alas, than I.

PISC. Well remembred, honest Scholar, I thank you
for these choice Verses, which I have heard formerly,
but had quite forgot, till they were recovered by your
happy memorie. Well, being I have now rested my self
a little, I will make you some requital, by telling you
some observations of the Eele, for it rains still, and
because (as you say) our *Angles* are as money put to

Use, that thrive when we play, therefore we'l sit still and injoy our selves a little longer under this *honey-suckle-hedg*.

Observations of the Eele, *and other fish that want scales, and how to fish for them.*

Pisc. It is agreed by most men, that the E*ele* is a most daintie fish; the Romans have esteemed her the *Hellena* of their feasts, and some *The Queen of pleasure.* But most men differ about their breeding: some say they breed by generation as other fish do, and others, that they breed (as some wormes do) of mud, as Rats and Mice, and many other living creatures are bred in *Egypt,* by the overflowing of the River N*ilus:* or out of the putrifaction of the earth, and divers other wayes. Those that deny them to breed by generation as other fish do, ask, if any man ever saw an E*ele* to have a Spawn or Melt? and they are answered, that they may be as certain of their breeding as if they had seen Spawn: for they say, that they are certain that E*eles* have all parts fit for generation, like other fish, but so small as not to be easily discerned, by reason of their fatness; but that discerned they may be, and that the He and the She E*ele* may be distinguished by their fins. And R*andeletius* saies, he has seen E*eles* cling together like D*ew-worms.*

And others say, that E*eles* growing old, breed other E*eles* out of the corruption of their own age, which Sir

Francis Bacon sayes, exceeds not ten years. And others say, that as *Pearles* are made of glutinous dew-drops, which are condensed by the Suns heat in those Countries, so *Eeles* are bred of a particular dew falling in the moneths of *May* or *June* on the banks of some particular Ponds or Rivers (apted by nature for that end) which in a few dayes is by the Suns heat turned into *Eeles,* and some of the Ancients have called the *Eels* that are thus bred, *The Off-spring of Jove.* I have seen in the beginning of *July,* in a River not far from *Canterbury,* some parts of it covered over with young *Eeles,* about the thickness of a straw; and these *Eeles,* did lie on the top of that water, as thick as motes are said to be in the Sun: and I have heard the like of other Rivers as namely in *Severn* (where they are called *Yelvers*) and in a *pond* or *mere* near unto *Stafford-shire,* where about a set time in Summer, such small *Eeles* abound so much, that many of the poorer sort of people that inhabit near to it, take such *Eeles* out of this Mere, with sieves or sheets, and make a kind of Eele-cake of them, and eat it like as bread. And *Gesner* quotes venerable *Bede* to say, that in *England* there is an Iland called *Ely,* by reason of the innumerable number of *Eeles* that breed in it. But that *Eeles* may be bred as some worms, and some kind of *Bees* and *Wasps* are, either of *dew,* or out of the corruption of the earth, seems to be made probable by the *Barnacles* and young *Goslings* bred by the Suns heat, and the rotten planks of an old Ship, and hatched of trees; both which are related for truths by *Dubartas* and

Lobel, and also by our learned *Cambden,* and laborious *Gerrard* in his *Herbal.*

It is said by *Randeletius,* that those *Eeles* that are bred in Rivers that relate to, or be nearer to the Sea, never return to the fresh waters (as the *Salmon* does alwayes desire to do) when they have once tasted the salt water; and I do the more easily believe this, because I am certain that powdered Beef is a most excellent bait to catch an *Eele*: and though Sir *Francis Bacon* will allow the *Eeles* life to be but ten years; yet he in his History of life and Death, mentions a *Lamprey* belonging to the *Roman* Emperour to be made tame, and so kept for almost threescore years: and that such useful and pleasant observations were made of this *Lamprey,* that *Crassus* the Orator (who kept her) lamented her death. And we read (in Doctor *Hackwel*) that *Hortensius* was seen to weep at the death of a *Lamprey* that he had kept long, and loved exceedingly.

It is granted by all, or most men, that *Eeles,* for about six moneths (that is to say, the six cold moneths of the year) stir not up and down, neither in the *Rivers* nor in the Pools in which they usually are, but get into the soft earth or mud, and there many of them together bed themselves, and live without feeding upon anything (as I have told you some *Swallowes* have been observed to do in hollow-trees for those six cold moneths), and this the *Eele* and *Swallow* do, as not being able to endure winter weather: For *Gesner* quotes *Albertus* to say, that in the year 1125 (that years winter being more cold then usually) E*eles* did by nature's instinct get out of the water into a stack of hay in a Meadow upon drie ground, and there bedded themselves, but yet at last a frost kil'd them. And our *Cambden* relates, that in *Lancashire* Fishes are dig'd out of the earth with Spades, where no water is near to the place. I shall say little more of the Eele, but that, as it is observed he is impatient of cold; so it hath been observed, that in warm weather an E*ele* has been known to live five dayes out of the water.

And lastly, let me tell you that some curious searchers into the natures of Fish, observe that there be several sorts or kinds of E*eles,* as the *silver* E*ele,* and green or *greenish* E*ele* (with which the River of T*hames* abounds, and those are called *Gregs*); and a *blackish* E*ele,* whose head is more flat and bigger than ordinary Eeles; and also an E*ele* whose Fines are reddish, and but seldome taken in this Nation, (and yet taken sometimes): These several kinds of E*eles* are (say some) diversly bred, as namely, out of the corruption of the earth, and by dew, and other wayes, (as I have said to you): and yet it is affirmed by some for a certain, that the *silver* E*ele* is bred by generation, but not by Spawning as other Fish do, but that her Brood come alive from her, little live Eeles no bigger nor longer than a pin; and I have had too many testimonies of this to doubt the truth of it my self, and if I thought it needful I might prove it, but I think it is needless.

And this Eele of which I have said so much to you,

may be caught with divers kinds of Baits; as namely with powdered Beef, with a *Lob* or *Garden-worm,* with a *Minnow,* or gut of a *Hen, Chicken,* or the guts of any Fish, or with almost anything, for he is a greedy Fish; but the Eele may be caught especially with a little, a very little *Lamprey,* which some call a *Pride,* and may in the hot moneths be found many of them in the River *Thames,* and in many mud-heaps in other Rivers, yea, almost as usually as one finds worms in a dunghill.

Next note, that the Eele seldom stirs in the day, but then hides himself, and therefore he is usually caught by night with one of these baits of which I have spoken, and then caught by laying hooks, which you are to fasten to the bank or twigs of a tree; or by throwing a string crosse the stream with many hooks at it, and baited with the aforesaid Baits, and a clod, or plummet, or stone, thrown into the River with this line, that so you may in the morning find it near to some fixt place, and then take it up with a Drag-hook or otherwise: but these things are indeed too common to be spoken of, and an hours fishing with any Angler will teach you better, both for these and many other common things in the practical part of *Angling,* than a weeks discourse. I shall therefore conclude this direction for taking the *Eele,* by telling you, that in a warm day in Summer I have taken many a good Eele by *snigling,* and have been much pleased with that sport.

And because you that are but a young Angler know not what snigling is, I will now teach it to you. You remember I told you that Eeles do not usually stir in the day-time, for then they hide themselves under some covert, or under boards or plancks about Floudgates, or Weires, or Mills, or in holes in the River banks; and you observing your time in a warm day, when the water is lowest, may take a strong small hook tied to a strong line, or to a string about a Yard long, and then into one of these holes, or between any boards about a Mill, or under any great stone or planck, or any place where you think an Eele may hide or shelter her self, there with the help of a short stick put in your Bait, but leasurely, and as far as you may conveniently; and it is scarce to be doubted, but that if there be an Eele within the sight of it, the Eele will bite instantly, and as certainly gorge it: and you need not doubt to have him if you pull him not out of the hole too quickly, but pull him out by degrees, for he lying folded double in his hole, will with the help of his tail break all, unlesse you give him time to be wearied with pulling, and so get him out by degrees; not pulling too hard.

And to commute for your great patience I shall next tell you how to make this Eele a most excellent dish of meat:

First, wash him in water and salt, then pull of his skin below his vent or navel, and not much further: having done that, take out his guts as clean as you can, but wash him not: then give him three or four scotches with a knife, and then put into his belly and those scotches sweet herbs, an Anchovy, and a little Nutmeg grated or cut very small, and your herbs and Anchovis must also be cut very small, and mixt with good Butter and salt: having done this, then pull his skin over him all but his head, which you are to cut off, to the end you may tie his skin about that part where his head grew, and it must be so tyed as to keep all his moisture within his skin: and having done this, tie him with Tape or Pack-thred to a spit, and rost him leasurely, and baste him with water and salt till his skin breaks, and then with Butter: and having rosted him enough, let what was put into his belly, and what he drips be his sawce. S. F.

But now let me tell you, that though the Eele thus drest be not onely excellent good, but more harmless than any other way, yet it is certain, that Physicians account the Eele dangerous meat; I will advise you therefore, as *Solomon* sayes of Hony, Prov. 25. *Hast thou found it, eat no more then is sufficient, lest thou surfeit, for it is not good to eat much honey.* And let me add this that the uncharitable *Italian* bids us, *Give Eels, and no wine to our enemies.*

And I will beg a little more of your attention to tell you that *Aldrovandus* and divers Physitians commend the Eele very much for medicine though not for meat. But let me tell you one observation, That the Eele is never out of season, as *Trouts* and most other fish are at set times, at least most Eeles are not.

I might here speak of many other Fish whose shape

and nature are much like the Eele and frequent both the *Sea* and fresh Rivers; as namely the *Lamprel,* the *Lamprey,* and the *Lamperne*; as also of the mighty *Congre,* taken often in *Severne,* about *Glocester,* and in what high esteem many of them are for the curiositie of their taste; but these are not so proper to be talk'd of by me, because they make us Anglers no sport, therefore I will let them alone as the Jewes do, to whom they are forbidden by their Law.

And Scholar, there is also a Flounder, a Sea-fish, which will wander very far into fresh Rivers, and there lose himself, and dwell and thrive to a hands breadth, and almost twice so long, a Fish without scales, and most excellent meat, and a Fish that affords much sport to the Angler, with any small worm, but especially a little blewish worm, gotten out of Marsh ground or Meadowes, which should be well scowred, but this though it be most excellent meat, yet it wants scales, and is as I told you therefore an abomination to the Jewes.

But Scholar, there is a fish that they in *Lancashire* boast very much of, called a *Char,* taken there (and I think there only) in a Mere called, *Winander Mere;* a Mere, sayes *Cambden,* that is the largest in this Nation, being ten miles in length, and as smooth in the bottom as if it were paved with pollisht marble: this fish never exceeds fifteen or sixteen inches in length; and 'tis spotted like a *Trout,* and has scarce a bone but on the back: but this, though I do not know whether it make the Angler sport, yet I would have you take notice of it, because it is a raritie, and of so high esteem with persons of great note.

Nor would I have you ignorant of a rare fish called a *Guiniad,* of which I shall tell you what *Cambden,* and others speak. The River *Dee* (which runs by *Chester*) springs in *Merionnithshire,* and as it runs toward *Chester,* it runs through *Pemble-Mere,* which is a large water: And it is observed, that though the River *Dee* abounds with *Salmon,* and *Pemble-Mere* with the *Guiniad,* yet there is never any *Salmon* caught in the *Mere,* nor a *Guiniad* in the River. And now my next observation shall be of the *Barbel.*

Observations of the Barbel, *and directions how to fish for him.*

Pisc. The B*arbel* is so called (saies G*esner*) by reason of his Barb or Wattels at his mouth, which are under his nose or chaps. He is one of those leather-mouthed Fish that I told you of, that very seldom break his hold if he be once hook'd: but he will often break both rod and line if he proves to be a big one.

But the B*arbel,* though he be of a fine shape, and looks big, yet he is not accounted the best fish to eat, neither for his wholsomness nor his taste: But the Male is reputed much better than the Female, whose Spawn is very hurtful, as I will presently declare to you.

They flock together like sheep, and are at worst in A*pril,* about which time they Spawn, but quickly grow to be in season. He is able to live in the strongest swifts of the Water, and in Summer loves the shallow-est and sharpest streams; and loves to lurk under weeds, and to feed on gravel against a rising ground, and will root and dig in the sands with his nose like a hog, and there nests himself: yet sometimes he retires to deep and swift Bridges, or Floud-gates, or Weires, where he will nest himself amongst piles, or in hollow places, and take such hold of mosse or weeds, that be the water never so swift, it is not able to force him from the place that he contends for. This is his constant custom in Summer, when he and most living creatures sport themselves in the Sun, but at the approach of Winter, then he forsakes the swift streams and shallow waters, and by degrees retires to those parts of the River that are quiet and deeper; in which places (and I think about that time) he Spawnes, and as I have formerly told you, with the help of the Melter, hides his Spawn or eggs in holes, which they both dig in the gravel, and then they mutually labour to cover it with the same sand, to prevent it from being devoured by other fish.

There be such store of this fish in the River *Danubie,* that *Randeletius* sayes, they may in some places of it, and in some moneths of the year, be taken by those that dwell near to the River, with their hands, eight or ten load at a time; he sayes, they begin to be good in *May,* and that they cease to be so in *August,* but it is found to be otherwise in this Nation: but thus far we agree with him, that the Spawn of a *Barbel,* if it be not poison as he sayes, yet that it is dangerous meat, and especially in the moneth of *May*; which is so certain that *Gesner* and *Gasius* declare, it had an ill effect upon them even to the indangering of their lives.

This fish is of a fine cast and handsome shape, small scales, and plac'd after a most exact and curious manner, and, as I told you, may be rather said not to be ill, then to be good meat; the *Chub* and he have (I think) both lost a part of their credit by ill cookery, they being reputed the worst or coursest of fresh-water-fish: but the *Barbel* affords an A*ngler* choice sport, being a lusty and a cunning Fish; so lusty and cunning as to endanger the breaking of the Anglers line, by running his head forcibly towards any covert, or hole, or bank: and then striking at the line, to break it off with his tail (as is observed by *Plutarch,* in his Book *De industria animalium*) and also so cunning to nibble and suck off your worm close to the hook, and yet avoid the letting the hook come into his mouth.

The *Barbel* is also curious for his baits, that is to say, that they be clean and sweet; that is to say, to have your worms well scowred, and not kept in sowre and musty moss, for he is a curious feeder; for at a well-scowred Lob-worm, he will bite as boldly as at any bait, and specially, if the night or two before you fish for him, you shall bait the places where you intend to fish for him with big worms cut into pieces: and note, that none did ever over-bait the place, nor fish too early or too late for a *Barbel.* And the *Barbel* will bite also at Gentles, which (not being too much scowred, but green) are a choice bait for him: and so is cheese, which is not to be too hard, but kept a day or two in a wet linnen cloth to make it tough: with this you may also bait the water a day or two before you fish for the *Barbel,* and be much the likelier to catch store; and if the cheese were laid in clarified honey a short time before (as namely, an hour or two) you were still the likelier to catch Fish: some have directed to cut the cheese into thin pieces, and toast it, and then tie it on the hook with fine silk: and some advise to fish for the *Barbel* with Sheeps tallow and soft cheese beaten or work'd into a Paste, and that it is choicely good in *August,* and I believe it: but doubtlesse the Lob-worm well scowred, and the Gentle not too much scowred, and cheese ordered as I have directed, are baits enough, and I think will serve in any moneth: though I shall commend any Angler that tries conclusions, and is industrious to improve the Art. And now, my honest Scholar, the long showre, and my tedious Discourse are both ended together: and I shall give you but this Observation, that when you fish for a *Barbel,* your Rod and Line be both long, and of good strength, for (as I told you) you will find him a heavy and a dogged fish to be dealt withal, yet he seldom or never breaks his hold if he be once strucken. And if you would know more of fishing for the *Umber* or *Barbel,* get into favour with Doctor *Shelden,* whose skill is above others; and of that the Poor that dwell about him have a comfortable experience.

And now lets go and see what interest the *Trouts* will pay us for letting our *Angle-rods* lie so long, and so quietly in the water for their use. Come, Scholar, which will you take up?

vena. Which you think fit, Master.

pisc. Why, you shall take up that; for I am certain by viewing the Line, it has a Fish at it. Look you, Scholar: well done. Come now, take up the other too: well, now you may tell my brother *Peter* at night, that you have caught a lease of *Trouts* this day. And now lets move toward our lodging, and drink a draught of *Red-Cowes Milk,* as we go, and give pretty *Maudlin* and her honest mother a brace of *Trouts* for their supper.

VENA. Master, I like your motion very well, and I think it is now about milking-time; and yonder they be at it.

PISC. God speed you, good woman, I thank you both for our Songs last night; I and my companion have had such fortune a fishing this day, that we resolve to give you and *Maudlin* a brace of *Trouts* for supper, and we will now taste a draught of your *Red-Cowes milk.*

MILKW. Marry, and that you shall with all my heart, and I will be still your debtor when you come this way: if you will but speak the word, I will make you a good *Sillabub,* of new Verjuice, and then you may sit down in a *haycock* and eat it, and *Maudlin* shall sit by and sing you the good old Song of the *Hunting in Chevy Chase,* or some other good Ballad; for she hath good store of them; *Maudlin,* my honest *Maudlin* hath a notable memory, and she thinks nothing too good for you, because you be such honest men.

VENA. We thank you, and intend once in a moneth to call upon you again, and give you a little warning, and so good night: good night, *Maudlin.* And now, good Master, lets lose no time; but tell me somewhat more of Fishing, and if you please, first something of Fishing for a *Gudgion.*

PISC. I will, honest Scholar.

Observations of the Gudgion, *the* Ruffe *and the* Bleak,
and how to fish for them.

THE *Gudgion* is reputed a Fish of excellent taste, and to be very wholsome: he is of a fine shape, of a silver colour, and beautified with black spots both on his body and tail. He breeds two or three times in the year, and alwayes in Summer. He is commended for a Fish of excellent nourishment: the *Germanes* call him *Groundling,* by reason of his feeding on the ground: and he there feasts himself in sharp streams, and on the gravel, He and the *Barbel* both feed so, and do not hunt for flies at any time, as most other Fishes do: he is an excellent fish to enter a young Angler, being easie to be taken with a small red worm, on or very near to the ground. He is one of those leather-mouthed fish that has his teeth in his throat and will hardly be lost off from the hook if he be once strucken: they be usually scattered up and down every River in the shallowes, in the heat of Summer: but in *Autumn,* when the weeds begin to grow sowre or rot, and the weather colder, then they gather together, and get into the deeper parts of the water: and are to be Fished for there, with your hook always touching the ground, if you Fish for him with a floate, or with a cork: But many will Fish for the *Gudgion* by hand, with a running line upon the ground, without a cork, as a *Trout* is Fished for, and it is an excellent way, if you have a gentle rod and as gentle a hand.

There is also another Fish called a *Pope*, and by some a *Ruffe*, a fish that is not known to be in some Rivers; it is much like the Pearch for his shape, and taken to be better than the Pearch, but it will not grow to be bigger than a Gudgion; he is an excellent Fish; no Fish that swims is of a pleasanter taste, and he is also excellent to enter a young *Angler*; for he is a greedy biter, and they will usually lie abundance of them together in one reserved place where the water is deep, and runs quietly, and an easie Angler, if he has found where they lie, may catch forty or fifty, or sometimes twice so many at a standing.

You must Fish for him with a small red-worm, and if you bait the ground with earth it is excellent.

There is also a *Bleak*, or fresh-water-Sprat, a Fish that is ever in motion, and therefore called by some the *River-Swallow*; for just as you shall observe the *Swallow* to be most evenings in Summer ever in motion, making short and quick turnes when he flies to catch Flies in the aire (by which he lives), so does the *Bleak* at the top of the water. *Ausonius* would have him called *Bleak* from his whitish colour: his back is of a pleasant sad or Sea-water-green, his belly white and shining as the Mountain snow; and doubtless though he have the fortune (which vertue has in poor people) to be neglected, yet the *Bleak* ought to be much valued, though we want *Allamot* salt, and the skill that the *Italians* have to turn them into Anchovis. This fish may be caught with a *Pater-noster* line, that is, six or eight very small hooks tyed along the line one half foot above the other: I have seen five caught thus at one time, and the bait has been Gentles, then which none is better.

Or this Fish may be caught with a fine small artificial flie, which is to be of a very sad brown colour, and very small, and the hook answerable. There is no better sport than whipping for *Bleaks* in a boat or on a banck, in the swift water in a Summers evening, with a Hazle top about five or six foot long, and a line twice the length of the Rod, I have heard Sir *Henry Wotton* say, that there be many that in *Italy* will catch *Swallows* so, or especially *Martins*, (the *Bird-angler* standing on the top of a Steeple to do it, and with a line twice so long as I have spoken of). And let me tell you, Scholar, that both *Martins* and *Bleaks* be most excellent meat.

And let me tell you, that I have known a Hern that did constantly frequent one place, caught with a hook baited with a big Minnow or a small *Gudgion*. The line and hook must be strong, and tied to some loose staff so big as she cannot flie away with it, a line not exceeding two Yards.

Is of nothing, or that which is nothing worth.

MY purpose was to give you some direction concerning *Roach* and *Dace*, and some other inferiour Fish, which make the Angler excellent sport; for you know there is more pleasure in hunting the Hare than in eating her: but I will forbear at this time to say any more, because you see yonder comes our brother *Peter* and honest *Coridon*: but I will promise you that as you and I fish and walk to morrow towards *London,* if I have now forgotten any thing that I can then remember, I will not keep it from you.

Well met, Gentlemen, this is lucky that we meet so just together at this very door. Come Hostess, where are you? is Supper ready? come, first give us drink, and be as quick as you can, for I believe we are all very hungry. Well, brother *Peter* and *Coridon*, to you both; come drink, and tell me *what luck of fish*: we two have caught but ten Trouts, of which my Scholar caught three; look here's eight, and a brace we gave away: we have had a most pleasant day for fishing and talking, and are returned home both weary and hungry, and now meat and rest will be pleasant.

PET. And *Coridon* and I have not had an unpleasant day, and yet I have caught but five Trouts: for indeed we went to a good honest Ale-house, and there we plaid at Shovel-board half the day; all the time that it rained we were there, and as merry as they that fished, and I am glad we are now with a dry house over our heads, for hark how it rains and blows. Come Hostess, give us more Ale, and our supper with what haste you may; and when we have sup'd, let us have your Song, P*iscator*, and the Ketch that your Scholar promised us, or else *Coridon* will be dogged.

PISC. Nay, I will not be worse than my word, you shall not want my Song, and I hope I shall be perfect in it.

VENA. And I hope the like for my Ketch, which I have already too, and therefore lets go merrily to supper, and then have a gentle touch at singing and drinking: but the last with moderation.

COR. Come, now for your Song, for we have fed heartily. Come Hostess, lay a few more sticks on the fire, and now sing when you will.

PISC. Well then, here's to you *Coridon*, and now for my Song.

Oh the gallant Fishers life,
It is the best of any,
'Tis full of pleasure, void of strife,
And 'tis belov'd of many:
Other joyes
are but toyes,
only this
lawful is,
for our skill

breeds no ill,
but content and pleasure.

In a morning up we rise,
Ere Aurora's *peeping,*
Drink a cup to wash our eyes,
Leave the sluggard sleeping:
Then we go
to and fro,
with our knacks
at our backs,
to such streams
as the Thames,
if we have the leasure.

When we pleas to walk abroad
For our recreation,
In the fields is our abode,
Full of delectation.
Where in a brook
with a book,
or a Lake,
fish we take;
there we sit,
for a bit,
till we fish intangle.

We have Gentles in a horn,
We have paste and worms too,
We can watch both night and morn,
Suffer rain and storms too:
None do here

use to swear,
oaths do fray
fish away,
we sit still,
and watch our quill;
Fishers must not rangle.

If the Suns excessive heat
  Make our bodies swelter,
To an Osier hedge we get
  For a friendly shelter,
    Where in a dike
    Pearch or Pike,
    Roach or Dace
    we do chase,
    Bleak or Gudgion
    without grudging,
we are still contented.

Or we sometimes pass an hour
  Under a green Willow,
That defends us from a showre,
  Making earth our pillow,
    There we may
    think and pray
    before death
    stops our breath:
    other joyes
    are but toyes,
and to be lamented.

Jo. Chalkhill.

VENA. Well sung, Master, this dayes fortune and pleasure, and this nights company and song, do all make me more and more in love with *angling*. Gentlemen, my Master left me alone for an hour this day, and I verily believe he retired himself from talking with me, that he might be so perfect in this song; was it not Master?

PISC. Yes indeed, for it is many Years since I learn'd it, and having forgotten a part of it, I was forced to patch it up by the help of mine own Invention, who am not excellent at Poetrie, as my part of the song may testifie: But of that I will say no more, lest you should think I mean by discommending it to beg your commendations of it. And therefore without replications lets hear your Ketch, Scholar, which I hope will be a good one, for you are both Musical, and have a good fancie to boot.

VENA. Marry and that you shall, and as freely as I would have my honest Master tell me some more secrets of fish and Fishing as we walk and fish towards *London* to morrow. But Master, first let me tell you, that, that very hour which you were absent from me, I sate down under a *Willow-tree* by the water side, and considered what you had told me of the Owner of that pleasant Meadow in which you then left me; that he had a plentiful estate, and not a heart to think so; that he had at this time many Law-suits depending; and that they both damp'd his mirth, and took up so much of his time and thoughts, that he himself had not leisure to take the sweet content that I (who pretended

no title to them) took in his fields; for I could there sit quietly, and looking on the water, see some Fishes sport themselves in the silver streams, others leaping at Flyes of several shapes and colours; looking on the Hills, could behold them spotted with Woods and Groves; looking down the Meadows, could see here a Boy gathering *Lillies* and *Lady-smocks*, and there a Girl cropping *Culverkeyes* and *Cow-slips*, all to make Garlands suitable to this present Moneth of *May*: these and many other Field-flowers, so perfumed the Air, that I thought that very Meadow like the Field in *Sicily* (of which *Diodorus* speaks) where the perfumes arising from the place, make all dogs that hunt in it, to fall off, and to lose their hottest sent. I say, as I thus sate joying in my own happy condition, and pitying this poor rich man, that owned this, and many other pleasant Groves and Meadows about me, I did thankfully remember what my Saviour said, that *the meek possess the earth*; or rather, they injoy what the other possess and injoy not; for Anglers and meek quiet-spirited-men, are free from those high, those restless thoughts which corrode the sweets of life; and they, and they onely can say as the Poet has happily exprest it:

> *Hail blest estate of lowliness!*
> *Happy enjoyments of such minds,*
> *As rich in self-contentednesse,*
> *Can, like the reeds in roughest winds*
> *By yielding make that blow but small*
> *At which proud Oaks and Cedars fall.*

There came also into my mind at that time, certain
Verses in praise of a mean estate, and an humble mind,
they were written by *Phineas Fletcher*: an excellent
Divine, and an excellent Angler, and the Author of
excellent Piscatory Eglogues, in which you shall see
the picture of this good mans mind.

> *No empty hopes, no Courtly fears him fright,*
> *No begging wants, his middle fortune bite,*
> But *sweet* content *exiles both* misery *and* spite.
> His *certain life, that never can deceive him,*
> *Is full of thousand sweets, and rich content:*
> *The smooth-leav'd* Beeches *in the field receive him,*
> *With coolest shade, till noon-tides heat be spent:*
> His *life is neither tost in boisterous Seas,*
> Or *the vexatious world, or lost in slothful ease;*
> Pleas'd *and ful blest he lives, when he his God can*
> *   please.*
>
> His *bed more safe than soft, yields quiet sleeps,*
> *While by his side his faithful Spouse has place,*
> His *little son into his bosom creeps,*
> *The lively picture of his fathers face.*
> His *bumble house, or poor state ne're torment him,*
> Less *he could like, if less his God had lent him,*
> And *when he dies, green turfs do for a tomb content*
> *   him.*

Gentlemen, these were a part of the thoughts that
then possest me, and I there made a conversion of a
piece of an old Ketch, and added more to it, fitting
them to be sung by us Anglers: come Master, you can

sing well, you must sing a part of it as it is in this paper.

The ANGLERS Song

For two voices: Trebble and Basse.   Set by Mr. *Henry Lawes.*

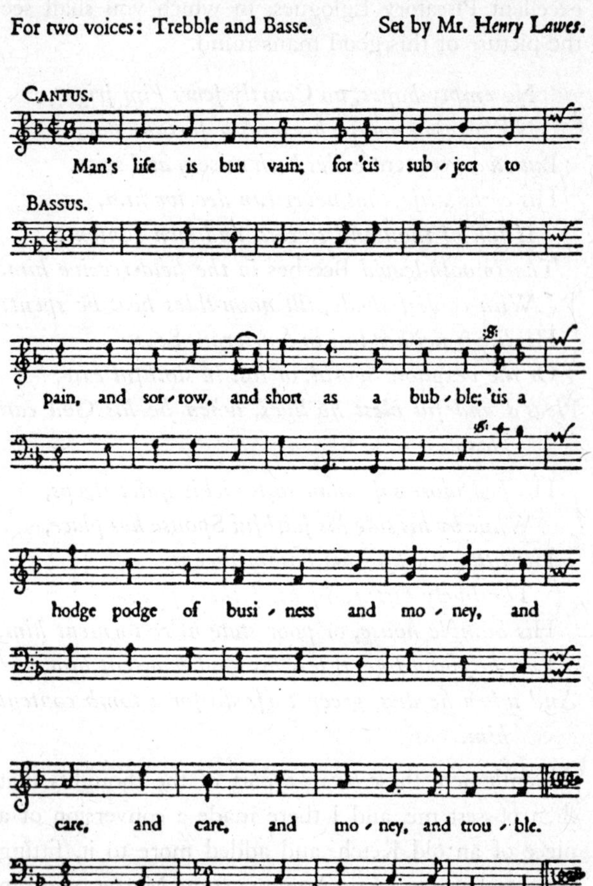

PET. I marry Sir, this is Musick indeed, this has cheer'd my heart, and made me to remember six Verses in praise of Musick, which I will speak to you instantly.

Musick miraculous Rhetorick, that speak'st sense
Without a tongue, excelling eloquence;

With what ease might thy errors be excus'd
Wert thou as truly lov'd as th' art abus'd?
But though dull souls neglect, and some reprove thee,
I cannot hate thee, 'cause the Angels love thee.

PISC. Well remembred brother P*eter*, these Verses came seasonably. Come, we will all joyn together, mine Hoste and all, and sing my Scholars Ketch over again, and then each man drink the tother cup and to bed, and thank God we have a dry house over our heads.

PISC. Well now, good night to every body.

PET. And so say I.

VENA. And so say I.

COR. Good night to you all, and I thank you.

PISC. Good morrow brother P*eter*, and the like to you honest *Coridon*: Come, my Hostesse sayes there is seven shillings to pay, let's each man drink a pot for his mornings draught, and lay down his two shillings, that so my Hostesse may not have occasion to repent her self of being so diligent, and using us so kindly.

PET. The motion is liked by every body, and so Hostesse, here's your money: we Anglers are all beholding to you, it will not be long e're I'll see you again. And now, brother P*iscator*, I wish you and my brother your Scholar a fair day, and good fortune. Come *Coridon*, this is our way.

Of Roach *and* Dace, *and how to fish for them.* And *of Cadis.*

VENA. Good Master, as we go now towards *London,* be still so courteous as to give me more instructions, for I have several boxes in my memory in which I will keep them all very safe, there shall not one of them be lost.

PISC. Well Scholar, that I will, and I will hide nothing from you that I can remember, and may help you forward towards a perfection in this Art, and because we have so much time, and I have said so little of *Roach* and *Dace,* I will give you some directions concerning them.

Some say the *Roach* is so called from *Rutilus,* which they say, signifies red fins: He is a Fish of no great reputation for his dainty taste, and his Spawn is accounted much better than any other part of him. And you may take notice, that as the *Carp* is accounted the *Water-fox,* for his cunning, so the *Roach* is accounted the *Water-sheep* for his simplicity or foolishness. It is noted that the *Roach* and *Dace* recovers strength, and grow in season in a fortnight after spawning, the *Barbel* and *Chub* in a moneth, the *Trout* in four moneths, and the *Salmon* in the like time, if he gets into the **Sea**, and after into fresh-water.

Roaches be accounted much better in the River than in a Pond, though ponds usually breed the biggest. But there is a kind of bastard small *Roach* that breeds in ponds with a very forked tail, and of a very small size, which some say is bred by the *Bream* and right *Roach*, and some Ponds are stored with these beyond belief; and knowing-men know their difference and call them *Ruds*: they differ from the true *Roach* as much as a Herring from a Pilchard, and these bastard breed of *Roach* are now scattered in many Rivers, but I think not in *Thames*, which I believe affords the largest and fattest in this Nation, especially below *London-Bridge*: the *Roach* is a leather-mouth'd Fish, and has a kind of saw-like teeth in his throat. And lastly let me tell you, the *Roach* makes an Angler excellent sport, especially the great Roaches about *London*, where I think there be the best Roach-Anglers, and I think that the best *Trout-Anglers* be in *Derbyshire*.

Next, let me tell you, you shall fish for this *Roach* in Winter with Paste or Gentles, in *April* with worms or Cadis; in the very hot moneths with little white snails, or with flies under-water, for he seldom takes them at the top, though the Dace will. In many of the hot moneths, Roaches may also be caught thus: Take a *May-fly* or *Ant-fly*, sink him with a little lead to the bottom near to the piles or posts of a Bridge, or near to any posts of a *Weire*, I mean any deep place where

Roaches lie quietly, and then pull your flie up very leisurely and usually a Roach will follow your bait to the very top of the water and gaze on it there, and run at it and take it lest the flie should flie away from him.

I have seen this done at *Windsor* and *Henly-Bridg*, and great store of *Roach* taken and sometimes a *Dace* or *Chub*; and in *August* you may fish for them with a Paste made onely of the crumbs of bread which should be of pure fine Manchet; and that must be so tempered betwixt your hands till it be both soft and tough too; a very little water and time and labour and clean hands will make it a most excellent paste: But when you fish with it, you must have a small hook, a quick eye, and a nimble hand, or the bait is lost and the fish too (if one may lose that, which he never had); with this paste, you may, as I said, take both the Roach and the Dace or Dare, for they be much of a kind, in matter of feeding, cunning, goodness, and usually in size. And therefore take this general direction for some other baits which may concern you to take notice of. They will bite almost at any flie, but especially at Antflies; concerning which, take this direction, for it is very good.

Take the blackish *Ant-flie* out of the Mole-hill or Ant-hill, in which place you shall find them in the moneth of *June*, or if that be too early in the year, then doubtlesse you may find them in *July*, *August*, and most of *September*, gather them alive with both their wings, and then put them into a glasse that will hold a quart or a pottle; but first put into the glasse a handful or more of the moist earth, out of which you gather them, and as much of the roots of the grass of the said hillock, and then put in the flies gently, that they lose not their wings, lay a clod of earth over it, and then so many as are put into the glasse without bruising, will live there a moneth or more, and be alwayes in a readinesse for you to Fish with; but if you would have them keep longer, then get any great earthen pot, or barrel of three or four gallons (which is better) then wash your barrel with water and honey; and having put into it a quantity of earth and grasse roots, then put in your flies, and cover it, and they will live a quarter of a year; these in any stream and clear water, are a deadly bait for *Roach* or *Dace*, or for a *Chub*, and your rule is, to Fish not lesse than a handful from the bottom.

I shall next tell you a winter bait for a *Roach*, a *Dace* or *Chub*, and it is choicely good. About *All-hollantide* (and so till Frost comes) when you see men ploughing up heath-ground, or sandy ground, or greenswards, then follow the plough, and you shall find a white worm as big as two Magots, and it hath a red head, (you may observe in what ground most are, for there the Crowes will be very watchful, and follow the Plough very close) it is all soft, and full of whitish guts; a worm that is in *Norfolk*, and some other Countries called a *Grub*, and is bred of the Spawn or Eggs of a Beetle, which she leaves in holes that she digs in the ground under Cow or Horse-dung, and there rests all Winter, and in *March* or *April* comes to be first a red, and then a black Beetle: gather a thousand or two of these, and put them with a peck or two of their own earth into some tub or firkin, and cover and keep them so warm, that the frost or cold air, or winds kill them not, and you may keep them all winter, and kill fish with them at any time: and if you put some of them into a little earth and honey a day before you use them, you will find them an excellent bait for *Bream* or *Carp*.

And after this manner you may also keep Gentles all winter, which is a good bait then, and much the better for being lively and tough: or you may breed and keep Gentles thus: Take a piece of Beasts liver, and with a cross stick, hang it in some corner over a pot or barrel half full of dry clay, and as the Gentles grow big, they will fall into the barrel and scowre themselves, and be alwayes ready for use whensover you incline to Fish; and these gentles may be thus made till after *Michaelmas*. But if you desire to keep Gentles to Fish with all the year, then get a dead Cat or a Kite and let it be fly-blown, and when the Gentles begin to be alive and to stir, then bury it and them in moist earth, but as free from frost as you can, and these you may dig up at any time when you intend to use them, these will last till *March*, and about that time turn to be Flies.

But if you be nice to foul your Fingers (which good Anglers seldom are) then take this Bait: Get a handful of well-made Mault, and put it into a dish of water, and then wash and rub it betwixt your hands till you make it clean, and as free from husks as you can; then put that water from it, and put a small quantitie of fresh water to it, and set it in something that is fit for that purpose over the Fire, where it is not to boil apace, but leasurely and very softly, until it become somewhat soft, which you may try by feeling it betwixt your Finger and Thumb, and when it is soft, then put your water from it, and then take a sharp Knife, and turning the sprout end of the Corn upward, with the point of your Knife take the back part of the husk off from it, and yet leaving a kind of inward husk on the Corn, or else it is marr'd, and then cut off that sprouted end, (I mean a little of it) that the white may appear, and so pull off the husk on the cloven side (as I directed you) and then cutting off a very little of the other end, that so your hook may enter, and if your hook be small and good, you will find this to be a very choice bait either for Winter or Summer, you sometimes casting a little of it into the place where your float swims.

And to take the R*oach* and D*ace,* a good Bait is the young brood of Wasps or Bees, if you dip their heads in blood; especially good for *Bream*, if they be baked or hardned in their husks in an Oven, after the bread is taken out of it, or on a Fire-shovel; and so also is the thick blood of *Sheep*, being half dried on a Trencher, that you may cut it into such pieces as may best fit the size of your hook, and a little salt keeps it from growing black, and makes it not the worst but better: This is taken to be a choice Bait if rightly ordered.

There be several Oiles of a strong smell that I have

been told of, and to be excellent to tempt Fish to bite, of which I could say much, but I remember I once carried a small Bottle from Sir *George Hastings* to Sir *Henry Wotton* (they were both chimical men) as a great Present; it was sent, and receiv'd, and us'd with great confidence; and yet upon inquiry I found it did not answer the expectation of Sir *Henry*, which with the help of this and other circumstances, makes me have little belief in such things as many men talk of: not but that I think Fishes both smell and hear (as I have exprest in my former discourse) but there is a mysterious Knack, which (though it be much easier than the Philosophers Stone, yet) is not attainable by common capacities, or else lies locked up in the brain or breast of some chimical man, that like the *Rosicrutians*, will not yet reveal it. But I stepped by chance into this discourse of Oiles and Fishes smelling, and though there might be more said, both of it and of Baits for *Roach* and *Dace*, and other float Fish, yet I will forbear it at this time, and tell you in the next place how you are to prepare your Tackling: concerning which I will for sport sake give you an old Rhime out of an old Fish-book, which will be a part of what you are to provide.

My Rod and my Line, my Float and my Lead,
My Hook and my Plummet, my whetstone and
    knife,
My Basket, my Baits both living and dead,
My Net and my Meat, for that is the chief:

*Then I must have Thred, and Hairs green and small,
With mine Angling purse, and so you have all.*

But you must have all these Tackling, and twice so many more, with which if you mean to be a Fisher, you must store your self;[1] and to that purpose I will go with you either to *Charles Brandons* (near to the *Swan* in *Golding-lane*) or to Mr. *Fletchers* in the Court which did once belong to Dr. *Nowel* the Dean of *Pauls*, he that I told you was a good man and a good Fisher; it is hard by the west end of St. *Pauls* Church. But if you will buy choice hooks, I will one day walk with you to *Charles Kerbyes* in *Harp-alley* in *Shoe-lane*, who is the most exact and best hook-maker the Nation affords. They be all three honest men, and will fit an Angler with what Tackling he wants.

VENA. Then, good Master, let it be at *Charls Brandons*, for he is nearest to my dwelling, and I pray let's meet there the ninth of *May* next, about two of the clock, and I'll want nothing that a Fisher should be furnished with.

PISC. Well, and I'll not fail you God willing, at the time and place appointed.

VENA. I thank you, good Master, and I will not fail you: and, good Master, tell me what Baits more you remember; for it will not now be long ere we shall be at *Tottenham-high-Cross*, and when we come thither I will make you some requital of your pains, by repeating as choice a copy of Verses, as any we have

---

[1] *I have heard, that the tackling hath been prized at fifty pounds in the Inventorie of an Angler.*

heard since we met together; and that is a proud word, for we have heard very good ones.

PISC. Well, Scholar, and I shall be right glad to hear them; and I will tell you whatsoever comes in my mind, that I think may be worth your hearing. You may make another choice Bait thus, Take a handful or two of the best and biggest W*heat* you can get, boil it in a little milk (like as *Frumity* is boiled), boil it so till it be soft, and then frie it very leisurely with Honey and a little beaten Saffron dissolved in milk, and you will find this a choice Bait, and good I think for any Fish, especially for *Roach, Dace, Chub,* or *Greyling*: I know not but that it may be as good for a River-*carp,* and especially if the ground be a little baited with it.

You are also to know, that there be divers kinds of *Cadis,* or *Caseworms,* that are to be found in this Nation in several distinct Counties, and in several little Brooks that relate to bigger Rivers, as namely, one *Cadis* called a *Piper,* whose husk or case is a piece of reed about an inch long or longer, and as big about as the compass of a two pence; these worms being kept three or four days in a woolen bag with sand at the bottom of it, and the bag wet once a day, will in three or four dayes turn to be yellow, and these be a choice Bait for the *Chub* or *Chavender,* or indeed for any great Fish, for it is a large Bait.

There is also a lesser *Cadis-worm,* called a *Cock-spur,* being in fashion like the spur of a Cock, sharp at one end, and the case or house in which this dwells is made of small husks and gravel, and slime, most curiously made of these, even so as to be woundred at, but not to be made by man no more than a *King-fishers* nest can, which is made of little Fishes bones, and have such a Geometrical inter-weaving and connexion, as the like is not to be done by the art of man: This kind of Cadis is a choice bait for any float-Fish, it is much less than the *Piper-Cadis*, and to be so ordered, and these may be so preserved ten, fifteen, or twenty days, or it may be longer.

There is also another *Cadis*, called by some a *Straw-worm*, and by some a *Ruff-coat*, whose house or case is made of little pieces of bents, and rushes, and straws, and water-weeds, and I know not what, which are so knit together with condensed slime, that they stick about her husk or case, not unlike the bristles of a *Hedg-hog*; these three *Cadis's* are commonly taken in the beginning of Summer, and are good indeed to take any kind of fish with float or otherwise. I might tell you of many more, which as these do early, so those have their time of turning to be flies later in Summer; but I might lose my self, and tire you by such a discourse, I shall therefore but remember you, that to know these, and their several kinds, and to what flies every particular *Cadis* turns, and then how to use them first as they be *Cadis*, and then as they be *flyes*, is an art, and an art that every one that professes to be an *Angler* has not leisure to search after, and if he had is not capable of learning.

Ile tell you, Scholar, several Countries have several kinds of *Cadisses*, that indeed differ as much as dogs do: That is to say, as much as a very *Cur* and a *Greyhound* do. These be usually bred in the very little rills or ditches that run into bigger Rivers, and I think a more proper bait for those very Rivers, than any other. I know not how or of what this *Cadis* receives life, or what coloured flye it turns to; but doubtlesse, they are the death of many Trouts, and this is one killing way.

Take one (or more if need be) of these large yellow *Cadis*, pull off his head, and with it pull out his black gut; put the body (as little bruised as is possible) on a very little hook, armed on with a Red hair (which will shew like the *Cadis-head*) and a very little thin lead, so put upon the shank of the hook that it may sink presently; throw this bait thus ordered (which will look very yellow) into a hole where a Trout is, and he will presently venture his life for it, 'tis not to be doubted if you be not espyed; and that the bait first touch the water, before the line, and this will do best in the stillest water.

Next let me tell you, I have been much pleased to walk quietly by a Brook with a little stick in my hand, with which I might easily take these, and consider the curiosity of their composure; and if you shall ever like to do so, then note, that your stick must be cleft, or have a nick at one end of it, by which means you may with ease take many of them in that nick out of the water, before you have any occasions to use them. These, my honest Scholar, are some observations told to you as they now come suddenly into my memory, of which you may make some use: but for the practical part, it is that that makes an Angler: it is diligence, and observation, and practice, and an ambition to be the best in the Art that must do it. I will tell you, Scholar, I once heard one say, I *envy not him that eats better* meat *than* I *do, nor him that is* richer, *or that wears better* clothes *than* I *do.* I *envy no body but him, and him only, that catches more* fish *than* I *do.* And such a man is like to prove an Angler, and this noble emulation I wish to you and all young Anglers.

Of *the* Minnow *or* Penk, *of the* Loach, *and of the*
Bull-head, *or* Millers-thumb.

Pᴵˢᶜ. There be also three or four other little fish that
I had almost forgot that are all without scales,
and may for excellency of meat be compared to any
fish of greatest value, and largest size. They be usually
full of eggs or spawn all the months of Summer; for
they breed often, as 'tis observed *mice* and many of the
smaller four-footed Creatures of the earth do; and as
those, so these come quickly to their full growth and
perfection. And it is needfull that they breed both often
and numerously, for they be (besides other accidents of
ruine) both a prey, and baits for other fish. And first,
I shall tell you of the *Minnow* or *Penk*.

The *Minnow* hath, when he is in perfect season, and
not sick (which is onely presently after spawning) a
kind of dappled or waved colour, like to a *Panther*, on
his sides, inclining to a greenish and skie-colour, his
belly being milk-white, and his back almost black or
blackish. He is a sharp biter at a small worm, and in
hot weather makes excellent sport for young Anglers,
or boyes, or women that love that Recreation, and in
the spring they make of them excellent *Minnow-Tan-
sies*; for being washed well in salt, and their heads and

tails cut off, and their guts taken out, they prove excellent for that use, being fryed with yolks of eggs, the flowers of *Cowslips*, and of *Primroses*, and a little *Tansie*.

The Loach is, as I told you, a most dainty fish, he breeds and feeds in little and clear swift brooks or rills; and lives there upon the gravel, and in the sharpest streams: He grows not to be above a finger-long, and no thicker than is suitable to that length. This *Loach*, is of the shape of the Eele: He has a beard or wattels like a *Barbel*. He has two fins at his sides, four at his belly and one at his tail; he is dapled with many black or brown spots, his mouth is Barbel-like under his nose. This Fish is usually full of eggs or spawn, and is by *Gesner* and other learned Physitians commended for great nourishment, and to be very grateful both to the palate and stomach of sick persons, and is to be fished for with a very small worm at the bottom, for he very seldom or never rises above the Gravel, on which I told you he usually gets his living.

The *Millers-thumb*, or *Bull-head*, is a Fish of no pleasing shape. He is by *Gesner* compared to the *Sea-toad-fish*, for his similitude and shape. It has a head big and flat, much greater than sutable to his Body; a mouth very wide and usually gaping. He is without teeth, but his lips are very rough, much like to a File. He hath two Fins near to his gills, which be roundish or crested, two Fins also under the Belly, two on the Back, one below the Vent, and the Fin of his tail is round. Nature hath painted the Body of this Fish with *whitish*, *blackish*, *brownish* spots. They be usually full of eggs or spawn all the Summer (I mean the Females) and those eggs swell their Vents almost into the form of a dug. They begin to spawn about *April*, and (as I told you) spawn several moneths in the Summer; and in the Winter the Minnow, and Loach, and Bull-head dwell in the mud as the Eele doth, or we know not where; no more than we know where the Cuckoe and Swallow, and other Summer-birds (which first appear to us in *April*) spend their cold winter melancholy moneths. This *Bull-head* does usually dwell and hide himself in holes or amongst stones in clear water; and in very hot daies will lie a very long time and very still, and sun himself, and will be easie to be seen upon any flat stone, or on any gravel, at which time he will suffer an Angler to put a hook baited with a small worm very near unto his very mouth, and he never refuses to bite, nor indeed to be caught with the worst of Anglers. *Matthiolus* commends him much more for his taste and nourishment, than for his shape or beauty.

There is also a little Fish called a *Sticklebag*; a Fish without scales, but hath his body fenc'd with several prickles. I know not where he dwells in winter, nor what he is good for in summer, but onely to make sport for boyes and women-Anglers, and to feed other Fish that be Fish of prey, as Trouts in particular, who will bite at him as at a Penk, and better, if your hook be rightly baited with him, for he may be so baited as his tail turning like the sail of a windmill will make him turn more quick than any *Penk* or *Minnow* can. For note, that the nimble turning of that or the *Minnow* is the perfection of *Minnow-fishing*. To which end, if you put your hook into his mouth, and out at his tail, and then having first tied him with white thred a little above his tail, and placed him after such a manner on your hook as he is like to turn, then sow up his mouth to your line, and he is like to turn quick, and tempt any *Trout*: but if he do not turn quick, then turn his tail a little more or lesse towards the inner part, or towards the side of the hook, or put the *Minnow* or *Sticklebag* a little more crooked or more strait on your hook, untill it will turn both true and fast; and then doubt not but to tempt any great *Trout* that lies in a swift stream. And the *Loach* that I told you of, will do the like; no bait is more tempting, provided the *Loach* be not too big.

And now *Scholar*, with the help of this fine morning, and your patient attention, I have said all that my present memory will afford me concerning most of the several Fish that are usually fisht for in fresh waters.

VENA. But Master, you have by your former civility made me hope that you will make good your promise, and say something of the several Rivers that be of most note in this Nation; and also of *Fish-ponds,* and the ordering of them; and do it I pray good Master; for I love any Discourse of Rivers, and Fish and fishing; the time spent in such discourse passes away very pleasantly.

Of several Rivers, *and some Observations of Fish.*

Pɪsc. Well Scholar, since the ways and weather do both favor us, and that we yet see not *Tottenham-Cross,* you shall see my willingness to satisfie your desire. And first, for the Rivers of this Nation, there be (as you may note out of Dr. H*eylins* Geography, and others) in number 325. but those of chiefest note he reckons and describes as followeth.

The chief is *Thamisis,* compounded of two Rivers, T*hame* and I*sis*; whereof the former rising somewhat beyond T*hame* in *Buckinghamshire,* and the latter in *Cyrencester* in *Glocestershire* meet together about *Dorcester* in *Oxfordshire*; the issue of which happy conjunction is the *Thamisis* or T*hames.* Hence it flyeth betwixt B*erks, Buckinghamshire, Middlesex, Surrey,* K*ent,* and E*ssex,* and so weddeth himself to the Kentish M*edway* in the very jaws of the Ocean; this glorious River feeleth the violence and benefit of the Sea more than any River in E*urope*; ebbing and flowing twice a day, more than sixty miles; about whose banks are so many fair Towns, and Princely Palaces, that a *German Poet* thus truly spake:

Tot Campos, &c.
We *saw so many* Woods *and Princely* bowers,

Sweet Fields, *brave* Palaces, *and stately* Towers,
So many Gardens *drest with curious care,*
That Thames *with* royal Tiber *may compare.*

2. The second River of note, is *Sabrina* or *Severn*; it hath its beginning in *Plinilimmon-Hill* in *Mont-gomery-shire*, and his end seven miles from *Bristol*, washing in the mean space the walls of *Shrewsbury*, *Worcester*, and *Glocester*, and divers other places and palaces of note.

3. *Trent*, so called for thirty kind of Fishes that are found in it, or for that it receiveth thirty lesser Rivers, who having his fountain in *Stafford-shire*, and gliding through the Countries of *Nottingham*, *Lincoln*, *Lei-cester*, and *York*, augmenteth the turbulent current of *Humber*, the most violent stream of all the Isle. This *Humber* is not, to say truth, a distinct River, having a spring head of his own, but rather the mouth or *Eus-torium* of divers Rivers here confluent and meeting to-gether; namely, your *Derwent*, and especially of *Ouse* and *Trent*; and (as the *Danow*, having received into its *channel*, the River *Dravus*, *Savus*, *Tibisnus*, and divers others) changeth his name into this of *Humber-abus*, as the old Geographers call it.

4. *Medway*, a Kentish River, famous for harbouring the Royal Navy.

5. *Tweed*, the north-east bound of *England*, on whose northern banks is seated the strong and impreg-nable Town of *Barwick*.

6. *Tine*, famous for *Newcastle*, and her inexhaust-

ible Coal-pits. These, and the rest of principal note, are thus comprehended in one of Mr. *Draytons* Sonnets.

The floods queen Thames *for ships and swans is*
　　crown'd,
　And stately Severn *for her shore is prais'd,*
The Chrystal Trent *for fords and fish renown'd,*
　And Avons *fame to* Albions *cliffs is rais'd,*

Carlegion Chester *vants her holy* Dee,
　York *many wonders of her* Ouse *can tell,*
The Peke *her* Dove, *whose banks so fertile be,*
　And Kent *will say her* Medway *doth excell.*

Cotswooll *commends her* Isis *to the* Tame,
　Our Northern borders boast of Tweeds *fair Flood,*
Our western parts extoll their Willies *fame,*
　And the old Lea *brags of the* Danish *blood.*

These observations are out of learned Dr. *Heylin,* and my old deceased friend *Michael Draiton*; and because you say, you love such discourses as these of *fish* and *fishing,* I love you the better, and love the more to impart them to you; nevertheless, *Scholar,* if I should begin but to name the several sorts of strange Fish that are usually taken in many of these Rivers that run into the Sea, I might beget wonder in you, or unbelief, or both; and yet I will venture to tell you a real truth concerning one lately dissected by Dr. *Wharton,* a man of great learning and experience, and of equall freedom to communicate it, one that loves me and my Art, one to whom I have been beholding for many of the choicest observations that I have imparted to you. This good man, that dares do any thing rather than tell an untruth, did (I say) tell me he lately dissected one, and he thus described it to me:

He was almost a yard broad, and twice that length; his mouth wide enough to receive or take into it the head of a man, his stomach seven or eight inches broad: he is of a slow motion, and usually lyes or lurks close in the mud, and has a moveable string on his head about a span, or near unto a quarter of a yard long, by the moving of which (which is his natural Bait) *when he lyes close and unseen in the mud, he draws other smaller fish close to him, and then sucks them into his mouth and devours them.*

And, Scholar, do not wonder at this; for besides the credit of the Relator, you are to note, many of these, and Fishes which are of the like and more usual shapes, are very often taken on the mouths of our Sea-rivers, and on the Sea-shore; and this will be no wonder to any that have travelled *Egypt,* where 'tis known the famous River *Nilus* does not onely breed Fishes that yet want names, but by the overflowing of that River by the help of the Suns heat on that fat slime which that River leaves on the Banks (when it falls back into its natural channel), strange Beasts are also bred, that no man can give a name to, as *Grotius* (in his *Sopham*) and others have observed.

But whither am I straid in this discourse? I will end it by telling you, that at the mouth of some of these Rivers of ours, Herrings are so plentiful, as namely, near to *Yarmouth* in *Norfolk*, and in the west Country, Pilchers so very plentiful, as you will wonder to read what our learned *Cambden* relates of them in his *Britannia*, p. 178, 186.

Well, Scholar, I will stop here, and tell you what by reading and conference I have observed concerning Fish-ponds.

Of Fish-ponds, and how to order them.

DOCTOR LEBAULT the learned French man, in his large discourse of *Mason Rustique*, gives this direction for making of *Fish-ponds*. I shall refer you to him to read it at large, but I think I shall contract it, and yet make it as useful.

He adviseth, that when you have dreined the ground, and made the earth firm where the head of the Pond must be, that you must then in that place drive in two or three rows of Oak or Elme Piles, which should be scorcht in the fire, or half burnt before they be driven into the earth (for being thus used preserves them much longer from rotting) and having done so, lay Fagots or Bavins of smaller wood betwixt them, and then earth betwixt and above them, and then having first very well rammed them and the earth, another pile used in like manner as the first were: and note that the second pile is to be of or about the height that you intend to make your Sluce or Flood-gate, or the vent that you intend shall convey the overflowings of your Pond in any flood that shall endanger the breaking of the Pond dam.

Then he advises that you plant Willows or Owlers about it, or cast in Bavins in some places not far from the side, and in the most sandy places for Fish both to spawn upon, and to defend them and the young Frie from the many Fish, and also from Vermin that lie at watch to destroy them, especially the spawn of the *Carp* and *Tench*. He and *Dubravius* and all others advise, that you make choice of such a place for your Pond, that it may be refresht with a little rill, or with rain water running or falling into it; by which Fish are more inclined both to breed, and are also refresht and fed the better, and do prove to be of a much sweeter and more pleasant taste.

To which end it is observed, that such Pools as be large and have most gravel, and shallows where *fish* may sport themselves, do afford Fish of the purest taste. And note, that in all Pools it is best for fish to have some retiring place, as namely hollow banks, or shelves, or roots of trees to keep them from danger; and when they think fit from the extream heat of Summer, as also from the extremity of cold in Winter. And note, that if many trees be growing about your Pond, the leaves thereof falling into the water, make it nausious to the Fish, and the Fish to be so to the eater of it.

'Tis noted that the *Tench* and *Eele* love mud, and the *Carp* loves gravelly ground, and in the hot moneths to feed on grasse: You are to cleanse your Pond if you intend either profit or pleasure, once every three or four Years (especially some Ponds) and then let them lie drie six or twelve moneths, both to kill the water-weeds, as *Water-lillies, Candocks, Reate,* and *Bull-*

rushes, that breed there; and also that as these die for want of water, so grasse may grow on the Ponds bottom, which *Carps* will eat greedily in all the hot moneths. The letting your Pond dry and sowing Oats in the bottom is also good, for the fish feed the faster: and being sometime let dry you may observe what kind of Fish either increases or thrives best in that water; for they differ much both in their breeding and feeding.

Lebault also advises, that if your Ponds be not very large and roomy, that you often feed your fish by throwing into them chippings of Bread, Curds, Grains, or the entrails of Chickens, or of any fowl or beast that you kill to feed your selves; for these afford Fish a great relief. He sayes that Frogs and Ducks do much harm, and devour both the Spawn and the young Frie of all Fish, especially of the *Carp*. And I have besides experience, many testimonies of it. But *Lebault* allows Water-frogs to be good meat, especially in some moneths, if they be fat: But you are to note, that he is a *Frenchman*, and we *English* will hardly believe him, though we know frogs are usually eaten in his Country: however he advises to destroy them and King-fishers out of your ponds; and he advises, not to suffer much shooting at wild fowle, for that (he saies) affrightens, and harms, and destroyes the Fish.

Note, that Carps and Tench thrive and breed best when no other Fish is put with them into the same Pond; for all other Fish devour their spawn, or at least the greatest part of it. And note, that clods of grass thrown into any Pond feed any Carps in Summer; and that garden earth and parsley thrown into a Pond, recovers and refreshes the sick fish. And note, that when you store your pond, you are to put into it two or three Melters for one Spawner, if you put them into a breeding Pond: but if into a nurse-pond, or feeding pond, in which they will not breed, then no care is to be taken, whether there be most Male or Female Carps.

It is observed, that the best ponds to breed Carps are those that be stonie or sandy, and are warm, and free from wind, and that are not deep, but have willow trees and grass on their sides, over which the water does sometimes flow: and note, that Carps do more usually breed in marle pits, or pits that have clean clay bottoms, or in new ponds, or ponds that lie dry a winter season, than in old ponds, that be full of mud and weeds.

Well *Scholar*, I have told you the substance of all that either *observation*, or *discourse*, or a diligent *Survey* of *Dubravius* and *Lebault* hath told me. Not that they in their long discourses have not said more, but the most of the rest are so common observations, as if a man should tell a good Arithmetician, that twice two is four. I will therefore end this discourse, and we will here sit down and rest us.

Directions for making of a Line, and for the colouring of both Rod and Line.

Pɪsᴄ. Well, Scholar, I have held you too long about these *cadis,* and smaller *fish,* and *rivers,* and *Fishponds,* and my spirits are almost spent, and so I doubt is your patience; but being we are now almost at *Tottenham,* where I first met you, and where we are to part, I will lose no time, but give you a little direction how to make and order your Lines, and to colour the hair of which you make your Lines, for that is very needfull to be known of an Angler; and also how to paint your Rod; especially your top, for a right grown top is a choice Commodity, and should be preserved from the water soaking into it, which makes it in wet weather to be heavy, and fish ill-favouredly, and not true, and also it rots quickly for want of painting: and I think a good top is worth preserving, or I had not taken care to keep a top above twenty years.

But first for your line.

First, note, That you are to take care, that your hair to be round and free from galls or scabs, or frets; for a well-chosen, even, clear, round hair, of a kind of glass-colour, will prove as strong as three uneven scabby hairs, that are ill chosen, and full of galls or unevenness. You shall seldom find a black hair but it is round, but many white are flat and uneven; therefore, if you get a lock of right, round, clear, glass-colour hair make much of it.

And for making your *Line*, observe this rule, First, let your hair be clean washt ere you go about to twist it: and then chuse not only the clearest hair for it, but hairs that be of an equal bigness, for such do usually stretch all together, and not break singly one by one, but all together.

When you have twisted your links lay them in water for a quarter of an hour, at least, and then twist them over again before you tie them into a Line; for those that do not so shall usually find their Lines to have a hair or two shrink, and be shorter than the rest at the first fishing with it, which is so much of the strength of the Line lost for want of first watering it, and then re-twisting it; and this is most visible in a seven-hair line, one which hath alwayes a black hair in the middle.

And for dying of your hairs do it thus:

Take a pint of strong Ale, half a pound of soot, and a little quantity of the juice of *Walnut*-tree leaves, and an equal quantity of Allome, put these together into a pot, or pan, or pipkin, and boil them half an hour, and having so done, let it cool, and being cold, put your hair into it, and there let it lie; it will turn your hair to be a kind of water or glass colour, or greenish, and the longer you let it lie, the deeper coloured it will be; you might be taught to make many other colours, but it is to little purpose; for doubtlesse the water or glass-coloured hair is the most choice and most useful for an *Angler*; but let it not be too green.

But if you desire to colour hair greener, then do it thus: Take a quart of small Ale, half a pound of Al-lome, then put these into a pan or pipkin, and your hair into it with them, then put it upon a fire and let it boil softly for half an hour, and then take out your hair, and let it dry, and having so done, then take a pottle of water, and put into it two handfull of Mary-golds, and cover it with a tile (or what you think fit), and set it again on the Fire, where it is to boil softly for half an hour, about which time the scum will turn yellow, then put into it half a pound of Copperas beaten small, and with it the hair that you intend to colour, then let the hair be boiled softly till half the liquor be wasted, and then let it cool three or four hours with your hair in it: and you are to observe, that the more Copperas you put into it, the greener it will be, but doubtlesse the pale green is best: But if you desire yellow hair (which is onely good when the weeds rot), then put in the more *Mary-golds,* and abate most of the Copperas, or leave it out, and take a little Verdigreece instead of it.

This for colouring your hair. And as for painting your Rod, which must be in Oil, you must first make a size with glue and water, boiled together, untill the glue be dissolved, and the size of a Lie-colour; then strike your size upon the wood with a Bristle, or a Brush or Pensil, whilst it is hot: that being quite dry, take white Lead, and a little red Lead, and a little cole black, so much as altogether will make an ash-colour; grind these all together with Linseed Oil, let it be thick, and lay it thin upon the wood with a Brush or Pensil, this do for the ground of any colour to lie upon wood.

For a Green.

Take Pink and Verdigreece, and grind them together in Linseed Oil, as thick as you can well grind it, then lay it smoothly on with your Brush, and drive it thin, once doing for the most part will serve, if you lay it well, and be sure your first colour be thoroughly dry before you lay on a second.

Well, Scholar, you now see *Tottenham*, and I am weary and therefore glad that we are so near it: and if I were to walk many more days with you, I could still be telling you more and more of the mysterious Art of Angling: But I will hope for another opportunity, and then I will acquaint you with many more, both necessary and true observations concerning fish and fishing: but now no more, let's turn into yonder Arbour, for it is a clean and cool place.

VENA. 'Tis a fair motion, and I will requite a part of your courtesies with a bottle of *Sack*, *Milk*, *Oranges*, and *Sugar*, which all put together, make a drink like *Nectar*, indeed too good for any body but us *Anglers*: and so Master, here is a full glasse to you of that liquor, and when you have pledged me, I will repeat the Verses which I promised you; it is a Copy printed amongst Sir *Henry Wottons* Verses, and doubtless made either by him, or by a lover of Angling: Come Master, now drink a glasse to me, and then I will pledge you, and fall to my repetition; it is a description of such *Country-Recreations* as I have enjoyed since I had the happiness to fall into your company.

Quivering fears, *heart-tearing* cares,
Anxious sighs, *untimely* tears,
  Flye, flye to Courts,
  Flye to fond worldlings sports,
Where strain'd Sardonick smiles are glosing still,
And grief is forc'd to laugh against her will.
  Where mirth's but mummery,
  And sorrows onely real be.

Flye from our Countrey-pastimes, flye,
Sad troops of humane misery,
  Come serene looks,
  Clear as the Christal Brooks,
Or the pure azur'd heaven that smiles to see
The rich attendance on our poverty;
  Peace and a secure mind,
  Which all men seek, we onely find.

Abused Mortals, *did you know*
Where joy, hearts-ease *and* comforts *grow,*
  You'ld scorne proud Towers,
  And seek them in these Bowers,
Where winds *sometimes our woods perhaps may*
    shake,
But blustring care *could never tempest make,*

Nor murmurs ere come nigh us,
Saving of fountains that glide by us.

Here's no fantastick Mask nor Dance,
But of our Kids that frisk and prance;
    Nor wars are seen,
    Unlesse upon the green
Two harmless Lambs are butting one the other,
Which done, both bleating, run each to his mother.
    And wounds are never found,
    Save what the plough-share gives the ground.

Here are no entraping baits
To hasten too too hasty fates,
    Unlesse it be
    The fond credulity
Of silly fish, which (worldling like) still look
Upon the bait, but never on the hook:
    Nor envy, 'nlesse among
    The birds for price of their sweet song.

Go, let the diving Negro seek
For Gems hid in some forlone creek:
    We all pearls scorne,
    Save what the dewy morne
Congeals upon each little spire of grasse,
Which carelesse shepherds beat down as they passe:
    And gold ne're here appears,
    Save what the yellow Ceres bears.

Blest silent groves, oh may you be
For ever mirths best nursery:

May pure contents
For ever pitch their tents
Upon these downs, these meads, these rocks, these
  mountains,
And Peace still slumber by these purling fountains:
Which we may every year
Meet when we come a fishing here.

PISC. Trust me (Scholar) I thank you heartily for these Verses, they be choicely good, and doubtless made by a lover of Angling: Come, now, drink a glass to me, and I will requite you with a very good Copy of Verses: it is a Farewell to the vanities of the World, and some say written by Sir *Harry Wootton,* who I told you was an excellent Angler. But let them be writ by whom they will, he that writ them had a brave soul, and must needs be possest with happy thoughts at the time of their composure:

Farewel ye gilded follies, pleasing troubles;
Farewell ye honour'd rags, ye glorious bubbles:
Fame's but a hollow eccho, Gold pure clay;
Honour the darling but of one short day.
Beauty (th' eyes idol) but a damask'd skin;
State but a golden prison, to live in,
And torture free-born minds; imbroydred Train
Meerly but pageants for proud swelling veins;
And Blood ally'd to Greatnesse is alone
Inherited, not purchas'd, nor our own.
  Fame, Honour, Beauty, State, Train, Blood, and
    Birth
  Are but the fading Blossoms of the earth.

I *would be* great, *but that the Sun doth still*
Level his rayes against the rising hill:
I *would be* high, *but see the proudest Oak*
Most subject to the rending Thunder-stroak:
I *would be* rich, *but see men (too unkind)*
Dig in the bowels of the richest mind:
I *would be* wise, *but that* I *often see*
The Fox suspected, whilest the Ass goes free:
I *would be* fair, *but see the fair and proud*
(Like the bright Sun) oft setting in a cloud.
I *would be* poor, *but know the humble grasse*
Still trampled on by each unworthy Asse:
Rich hated: wise suspected: scorn'd if poor:
Great fear'd: fair *tempted:* high *still envy'd more:*
　I *have wish'd all; but now* I *wish for neither;*
　Great, high, rich, wise, *nor* fair; poor I*le be rather.*

Would the world now adopt me for her heir,
Would Beauties Queen entitle me the Fair,
Fame speak me Fortunes Minion: *could* I *vie*
Angels with India, *with a speaking eye*
Command bare heads, bow'd knees, strike Justice
　dumb
As well as blind and lame, or give a tongue
To stones by Epitaphs: be call'd great Master
In the loose Rhimes of every Poetaster:
　Could I *be more than any man that lives,*
Great, fair, rich, wise, in all Superlatives:
Yet I *more freely would these gifts resign,*
Than ever fortune would have made them mine,

And hold one minute of this holy leasure
Beyond the riches of this empty pleasure.

Welcome pure thoughts, welcome ye silent Groves,
These guests, these courts my soul most dearly loves:
Now the wing'd people of the skie shall sing
My cheerful Anthems to the gladsom Spring:
A Pray'r-Book now shall be my looking-glass,
In which I will adore sweet Vertue's face.
Here dwell no hateful looks, no Palace-cares,
No broken Vows dwell here, nor pale-fac'd Fears:
Then here I'll sit and sigh my hot loves folly,
And learn t' affect a holy melancholy,
  And if Contentment be a stranger then,
  I'll ne're look for it, but in heaven agen.

VENA. Well Master, these Verses be worthy to keep a room in every mans memory. I thank you for them; and I thank you for your many instructions, which (God willing) I will not forget: and as St. *Austin* in his Confessions (book 4. chap. 3.) commemorates the kindness of his friend *Verecundus*, for lending him and his companion a *Country-house*, because there they rested themselves from the troubles of the world; so I having had the like advantage, both by your conversation, and the Art you have taught me, ought ever to do the like: for indeed your company and discourse have been so useful and pleasant, that I may truly say, *I have only lived since I enjoyed them, and turned Angler, and not before.* Nevertheless, here I must part with you, here in this now sad place where I was so happy as first to meet you; But I shall long for the ninth of *May*, for then I hope again to enjoy your beloved company, at the appointed time and place. And now I wish for some somniferous potion, that might force me to sleep away the intermitted time, which will passe away with me as tediously, as it does with men in sorrow; nevertheless I will make it as short as I can by my *hopes* and *wishes*. And, my good Master, I will not forget the doctrine which you told me *Socrates* taught his Scholars, *That they should not think to be honoured so much for being* Philosophers *as to honour* Philosophie *by their vertuous lives*. You advised me to the like concerning *Angling*, and I will endeavour to do so, and to live like those many *worthy men,* of which you made mention in the former part of your Discourse. This is my firm resolution, and as a pious man advised his friend, *That to beget* Mortification *he should frequent* Churches, *and view* Monuments, *and* Charnel-houses, *and then and there consider, how many dead bones time had piled up at the gates of death.* So when I would beget *content,* and increase confidence in the *Power,* and *Wisdom,* and *Providence* of Almighty God, I will walk the *Meadows* by some gliding stream, and there contemplate the *Lillies* that take no care, and those very many other various little living *creatures* that are not onely created but fed (man knowes not how) by the goodness of the God of *Nature.* This is my purpose, and so, *Let every thing that hath breath praise the* Lord. And let the blessing of St. *Peters* Master be with mine.

 PISC. And upon all that are lovers of **Vertue**, and all that love to be quiet, and go a *fishing*.

 Study to be quiet, 1 Thes. 4. 11.

A SHORT
DISCOURSE
BY WAY OF POST-SCRIPT
TOUCHING THE
LAWES OF ANGLING

My Good Friend,

I cannot but tender my particular thanks to you, for that you have been pleased by three Editions of your *Complete Angler,* freely to dispense your dear-bought Experiences to all the lovers of that Art; and have thereby so excellently vindicated the Legality thereof as to Divine approbation, that if I should go about to say more in that behalf, it indeed were to light a Candle to the Sun: But since all pleasures (though never so innocent in themselves) lose that stamp, when they are either pursued with inordinate affections, or to the prejudice of another; therefore as to the former, every man ought to endeavour, through a serious consideration of the vanity of worldly contentments, to moderate his affections thereunto, whereby they may be made of excellent use, as some poisons allayed are in Physick: And as to the latter, we are to have recourse to the known Laws, ignorance whereof excuseth no man, and by their directions so square our actions, that we hurt no man, but keep close to that

265

golden Rule, To *do to all men, as we would our selves be done unto.*

Now concerning *the Art of Angling,* we may conclude, Sir, that as you have proved it to be of great Antiquity, so I find it favoured by the Laws of this Kingdom; for where provision is made by our Statutes *primo Elizab. cap.* 17. against taking Fish by Nets that be not of such and such a size there set down, yet those Law-makers had so much respect to Anglers, as to except them, and leave them a liberty to catch as big as they could, and as little as they would catch. And yet though this Apostolical Recreation be simply in it self lawful, yet no man can go upon another mans ground to fish, without his license, but that he is a Trespasser; but if a man have license to enter into a Close or Ground for such a space of time, there, though he practise Angling all that time, he is not a Trespasser, because his Fishing is no abuse of his license; but this is to be understood of Running Streams, and not of Ponds or standing Pools; for in case of a Pond or standing Pool, the Owner thereof hath a property in the fish, and they are so far said to be his, that he may have Trespass for the fish against any one that shall take them without his license, though it be upon a Common, or adjoyning to the Kings High-way, or adjoyning to another mans ground, who gives license: But in case of a River, where one or more have *libera piscaria,* only it is otherwise, for there the fishes are said to be *ferae naturae,* and the taking of them with an Angle is not Trespasse, for that no man is said to have a property in them till he have caught them, and then it is a Trespass for any to take them from him: but this is not to be understood of fishes confined to a mans own ground by grates or otherwise, so that they cannot pass away, but may be taken out or put in at pleasure, for in that case the party hath a property in them, as in the case of a standing Pool.

But where any one hath *separabilis piscaria,* as in *Child* and *Greenhills* Case[1] in *Trin.* 15. *Car.* 1. in the Kings Bench, there it seemeth that the fish may be said to be his, because no man else may take them whilest they are within his several fishing; therefore what is meant by a several fishing is necessary to be considered: and though the difference between a Free fishing and a Several fishing be often treated of in the ancient books of the Law, and some Opinions will have the difference to be great, and others small or nothing at all; yet the certainest definition of a several fishing is, where one hath the Royalty, and owneth the ground on each side of the water: which agreeth with Sir *William Calthropps* Case,[2] where an Action was brought by him against another for fishing in his several fishing, &c., to which the Defendant pleaded, That the place wherein the Trespass was supposed to be done, contained ten Perches of Land in length, and twenty Perches in breadth, which was his own Freehold at the time when the Trespasse was supposed to be done, and that he fished there as was lawful for him

[1] Tr. 15. Car. 1.
[2] Mich. 17. E. 4. 6. and Pasc. 18. E. 4. 4.

to do: and this was adjudged a good Plea by the whole
Court, and upon argument in that very Case it was
agreed, that no man could have a several fishing but
in his own soyl, and that free fishing may be in the
soyl of another man, which was all agreed unto by *Lit-
tleton* our famous English Lawyer. So that from all
this may be drawn this short conclusion, That if the
Angler take care that he offend not with his feet, there
is no great danger of his hands.

But there are some covetous rigid persons, whose
souls hold no sympathy with those of the innocent An-
glers, having either got to be Lords of Royalties, or
owners of Lands adjoyning to Rivers, do, by some
apted clownish nature and education for the purpose,
insult and domineer over the innocent Angler, beating
him, breaking his Rod, or at least taking it from him,
and sometimes imprisoning his person as if he were a
Felon: Whereas a true-bred Gentleman scorns those
spider-like attempts, and will rather refresh a civil
stranger at his Table, than warn him from coming on
his ground upon so innocent an occasion. It would
therefore be considered how far such furious drivers
are warranted by the Law, and what the Angler may
(in case of such violence) do in defence of himself: If
I come upon another mans ground without his license,
or the license of the Law, I am a Trespasser, for which
the owner may have an Action of Trespasse against
me, and if I continue there after warning to depart by
the owner, or his servant thereunto authorized, the
owner or his servant by his command, may put me off

by force, but not beat me, but in case of resistance by me, for then I (by resisting) make the assault; but if he beat me, I not resisting, in that case he makes the assault, and I may beat him in defence of my self, and to free my self from his violence: and in case I shall leave my Rod behind in his ground, he may take it damage feasant, but he can neither take it from my person by force, nor break it, but he is a Trespasser to me: Which seems clear by the case of *Reynell* and *Champernoon*,[1] where *Reynell* brought an Action of Trespass against *Champernoon* for taking and cutting his Nets, the Defendant justified for that he was seised in fee of a several fishing, and that the Plaintiff with others endeavoured to rowe upon his water, and with the nets to catch his fish, and that for the safe-guard of his fishing he took and cut the Nets and Oars; to which plea the Plaintiff demurred; and there it was adjudged by the whole Court, that he could not by such colour cut the Nets and Oars, and judgment was thereupon given for the Plaintiff.

Doubtless our Fore-fathers well considered, that man to man was a wolf, and therefore made good Laws to keep us from devouring one another, and amongst the rest a very good Statute was made in the three and fortieth year of Queen *Elizabeth,* whereby it is provided, that in personal Actions in the Courts at *Westminster* (being not for Land or Battery), when it shall appear to the Judges (and be so by them signified) that the debt or damages to be recovered amount

[1] Mich. 7. Car. 1.

not to the sum of forty shillings or above, the said Judges shall award to the Plaintiff no more costs than damages, but lesse at their discretion.

And now with my acknowledgment of the advantage I have had both by your friendship and your book, I wish nothing that looks like an alteration in the first, nor any thing in the last, but that, by reason of the useful pleasure of it, you had called it *The Arcadia of Angling,* for it deserves that Title, and I would deserve the continuance of your Friendship.

FINIS

THE CHIEF

ALTERATIONS AND ADDITIONS

IN THE FIFTH EDITION

OF 1676

The text of The Compleat Angler *has been printed here from the fourth edition of 1668. The Second Part by Charles Cotton was added to the fifth edition of 1676, in which the First Part was also carefully revised by the author. The principal alterations and additions made by Walton in the fifth edition are as follows:*

CHAPTER I

P. 39, l. 20. *Suns heat, but*] 1676 *has*: "suns's heat, she flies so near it, but. . . ."

P. 46, l. 21. *his sent*] 1676 *has*: "his first scent. . . ."

P. 50, l. 19. *Physician*] 1676 *adds*: "Dr. Wharton. . . ."

P. 51, l. 16. *Learning*] 1676 *adds*: "must be pleasing."

P. 52, l. 4. *such things have*] 1676 *has*: "such things ever were, or that any of them have. . . ."

P. 53, l. 15. *is an Art*] 1676 *adds*: "is it not an art to deceive a Trout with an artificial Fly? a Trout! that is more sharp-sighted than any Hawk you have named, and more watchful and timorous than your high-mettled Marlin is bold? and yet, I doubt not to catch

271

a brace or two to-morrow, for a friend's breakfast: doubt not therefore, Sir, but that angling is an art. . . ."

P. 53, l. 20. *practice and experience*] 1676 *has*: "discourse and practice. . . ."

P. 57, l. 16. *there be divers wonders reported of them*] 1676 *has*: "there be so many wonders reported and written of them, and of the several creatures that be bred and live in them, and those. . . ."

P. 58, l. 15. *Sabbath*] 1676 *adds*: "But I will lay aside my discourse of rivers, and tell you some things of the monsters, or fish, call them what you will, that they breed and feed in them. Pliny the philosopher says (in the third chapter of his ninth book) that in the Indian Sea, the fish called the Balaena or Whirlpool, is so long and broad, as to take up more in length and breadth than two acres of ground; and, of other fish of two hundred cubits long; and that in the river Ganges, there be Eels of thirty foot long. He says there, that these monsters appear in that sea only, when the tempestuous winds oppose the torrents of waters falling from the rocks into it, and so turning what lay at the bottom to be seen on the water's top. And he says, that the people of Cadara, an island near this place, make the timber for their houses of those fishbones. He there tells us, that there are sometimes a thousand of these great Eels found wrapt, or interwoven together. He tells us there, that it appears that dolphins love music, and will come, when called for, by some men or boys, that know and use to feed them; and that they can swim as swift as an arrow can be shot out a bow; and much of this is spoken concerning the dolphin, and other fish, as may be found also in learned Dr. Casaubon's *Discourse of Credulity and Incredulity*, printed by him about the year 1670.

"I know, we Islanders are averse to the belief of these wonders; but there be so many strange creatures to be now seen, many collected by John Tredescant, and others added by my friend Elias Ashmole, Esq., who now keeps them carefully and methodically at his house near to Lambeth, near London, as may get some belief of some of the other wonders I mentioned. I will tell you some of the wonders that you may now see, and not till then believe, unless you think fit.

"You may there see the Hog-fish, the Dog-fish, the Dolphin, the Cony-fish, the Parrot-fish, the Shark, the Poison-fish, Sword-fish, and not only other incredible fish, but you may there see the Salamander, several sorts of Barnacles, of Solan Geese, the Bird of Paradise, such sorts of Snakes, and such Bird's-nests, and of so various forms, and so wonderfully made, as may beget wonder and amusement in any beholder: and so many hundred of other rarities in that collection, as will make the other wonders I spake of, the less incredible; for, you may note, that the waters are Nature's storehouse, in which she locks up her wonders."

P. 64, l. 12. *Gentiles*] 1676 *adds*: "and inspired them also with a power to speak all languages, and by their powerful eloquence to beget faith in the unbelieving Jews; and themselves to suffer for that Saviour whom their forefathers and they had crucified; and, in their sufferings, to preach. . . ."

P. 66, l. 10. *him*] 1676 *has*: "Amos. . . ."

P. 67, l. 5. *a toilsom*] 1676 *has*: "a turbulent, toilsome. . . ."

CHAPTER II

P. 75, l. 17. *in a night*] 1676 *adds*: "to catch for her young ones, or to glut herself with fish, and I can tell you that Pigeons will fly forty miles for a breakfast. . . ."

P. 77, l. 26. *like mine hoste*] 1676 *has*: "like your lodging, and mine host. . . ."

CHAPTER III

P. 85, l. 10. *the Chub to be*] 1676 *has*: "the Chub being dressed in the blood and quickly, to be. . . ."

P. 85, l. 11. *labour*] 1676 *adds*: "and disabuse your opinion."

P. 85, l. 29. *gutted*] 1676 *adds*: "as indeed no fish should be."

P. 88, l. 18. *skin*] 1676 *adds*: "of the mouth. . . ."

CHAPTER IV

P. 93, l. 9. *that there is a Fish . . . no man knows what*] 1676 *has instead*: "that grasshoppers and some fish have no mouths, but are nourished and take breath by the porousness of their gills, man knows not how; and this may be believed, if we consider that when the raven hath hatched her eggs, she takes no further care, but leaves her young ones to the care of the God of nature, who is said, in the *Psalms*, 'to feed the young ravens that call upon him.' And they be kept alive and fed by a dew, or worms that breed in their nests, or some other ways that we mortals know not. . . ."

P. 93, l. 28. *swallows*] 1676 *adds*: "and bats and wagtails. . . ."

P. 93, l. 29. *which are*] 1676 *adds*: "called half-year birds, and. . . ."

P. 97, l. 5. *Trouts, though they all go*] 1676 *has*: "Trouts, but these several kinds are not considered but by very few men, for they go. . . ."

P. 97, l. 6. *just as there be*] 1676 *has*: "just as pigeons do in most places; though it is certain, there are. . . ."

P. 97, l. 7-8. (*and too many to name*) *which all differ, and so do Trouts in their bignesse, shape and colour*] 1676 *has*: "and indeed too many to name. Nay, the Royal Society have found and published lately, that there be thirty and three kinds of spiders; and yet all, for aught I know, go under that one general name of Spider. And 'tis so with many kinds of fish, and of Trouts especially; which differ in their bignesse and shape, and spots and colour."

P. 99, l. 2. *high hedge: We'll sit*] 1676 *has*: "high honeysuckle hedge; there we'll sit and sing. . . ."

P. 99, l. 26. *that had cast away all care*] 1676 *has*: "that had not yet attained so much age and wisdom as to load her mind with any fears of many things that will never be, as too many men too often do; but she cast away all care. . . ."

P. 101, l. 2. *Chevy Chase*] 1676 *adds*: "or Johnny Armstrong, or Troy Town?"

P. 104, l. 24. *at the end of "The Milk-Maids Mothers Answer"*] 1676 *adds*: "MOTHER. Well, I have done my song. But stay, honest anglers; for I will make Maudlin to sing you one short song more. Maudlin! sing that song that you sung last night, when young Coridon the shepherd played so purely on his oaten pipe to you and your cousin Betty.

MAUDLIN. I will, mother.

> I married a wife of late,
> The more's my unhappy fate:
> I married her for love,
> As my fancy did me move,
> And not for a worldly estate:
> But oh! the green-sickness
> Soon changed her likeness;
>
> And all her beauty did fail.
> But 'tis not so
> With those that go
> Thro' frost and snow,
> As all men know,
> And carry the milking-pail."

CHAPTER V

P. 105, l. 15-16. *if the weather be anything like*] 1676 *has*: "for I'll be early up."

P. 108, l. 2-3. *and merry too*] 1676 *has*: "and as merry as beggars."

P. 124, l. 28. *and a good hook lost*] 1676 *adds*: "VENATOR. Aye, and a good Trout too.

PISCATOR. Nay, the Trout is not lost; for pray take notice, no man can lose what he never had."

P. 138, l. 14. *Clora*] 1676 *has*: "Kenna. . . ."

P. 141, l. 21. *and none*] 1676 *has*: "and so loud that not one. . . ."

P. 141, l. 30. *at night*] 1676 *adds*: "for he was an upright judge. . . ."

P. 144, l. 12. *belief*] 1676 *adds*: "And to make the wonder seem yet less that hares change sexes, note that Dr. Mer. Casaubon affirms, in his book of credible and incredible things, that Gaspar Peucerus, a learned physician, tells us of a people that once a year turn wolves, partly in shape, and partly in conditions."

P. 146, l. 8. *colour*] 1676 *adds*: "and at the snap. . . ."

CHAPTER VI

P. 151, l. 6. *a Grayling*] 1676 *has*: "an Umber or Grayling. . . ."

P. 152, l. 8. *fishes in Trent*] 1676 *has*: "fishes in the delicate river Dove, and in Trent. . . ."

CHAPTER VII

P. 154, l. 12. *gristle*] 1676 *adds*: "which shows him to be kipper. . . ."

P. 155, l. 14. *friend*] 1676 *adds*: "as he tells it you, in his *Polyalbion*. . . ."

P. 156, l. 3. *after the verses*] 1676 *adds*: "This Michael Drayton tells you of this leap or somersault of the Salmon."

P. 158, l. 8. *fresh Moss*] 1676 *adds*: "and some advise to put camphire into it."

P. 159, l. 10. *hear*] 1676 *adds*: "and, doubtless, can more probably smell. . . ."

Chapter VIII

P. 163, l. 20. *poison*] 1676 *adds*: "And he has a strange heat, that though it appear to us to be cold, can yet digest or put over any fish flesh, by degrees, without being sick."

P. 167, l. 27. *living bait*] 1676 *adds*: "though a dead one may catch. . . ."

P. 174, l. 17. *for him*] 1676 *adds*: "and to dress him, but not till he is caught."

Chapter IX

P. 178, l. 13. *devoured*] 1676 *adds*: "And a person of honour, now living in Worcestershire (Mr. Fr. Ru.) assured me he had seen a necklace or collar of tadpoles hang like a chain or necklace of beads about a Pike's neck, and to kill him; whether it were for meat or malice, must be to me a question."

P. 184, l. 4. *serve it up*] 1676 *adds*: "And much good do you!"

Chapter X

P. 185, l. 22. *warm*] 1676 *adds*: "and fresh water got into the pond, he affirms. . . ."

P. 191, l. 11. *out of the water*] 1676 *adds*: "at his appearance. . . ."

Chapter XIII

P. 202, l. 3. *Queen of pleasure*] 1676 *has*: "queen of palate-pleasure. . . ."

P. 132, l. 2. *by the overflowing*] 1676 *has*: "by the sun's heat when it shines upon the overflowing. . . ."

P. 207, l. 22. *great patience*] 1676 *has*: "patient hearing this long direction. . . ."

P. 208, l. 12. *sauce* S.F.] 1676 *adds*: "When I go to dress an Eel thus, I wish he were as long and big as that which was caught in Peterborough river in the year 1667; which was a yard and three-quarters long. If you will not believe me, then go and see at one of the coffeehouses in King Street in Westminster."

Chapter XVI

P. 228, l. 4. *after the verses*] 1676 *adds*:
"VENATOR. And the repetition of these last verses of music have called to my memory what Mr. Ed Waller, a lover of the angle, says of love and music:

> Whilst I listen to thy voice,
>   Chloris! I feel my heart decay;
>   That powerful voice
>   Calls my fleeting soul away:
>   Oh! suppress that magic sound,
>   Which destroys without a wound.
>
> Peace, Chloris! peace, or singing die,

That together you and I
To Heaven may go;
For all we know
Of what the blessed do above,
Is, that they sing, and that they love."

P. 228, l. 6. *seasonably*] 1676 *adds*: "and we thank you heartily."

CHAPTER XVII

P. 230, l. 20. *Derbyshire*] 1676 *adds*: "for the waters there are clear to an extremity."

P. 233, l. 9. *Carp*] 1676 *adds*: "or indeed for almost any fish."

P. 235, l. 16. *reveal it*] 1676 *adds*: "But let me nevertheless tell you, that camphire put with moss into your worm-bag with your worms, makes them (if many anglers be not very much mistaken) a tempting bait, and the angler more fortunate."

P. 235, l. 23. *will be a part*] 1676 *has*: "will prove a part, and but a part. . . ."

P. 236, l. 6-14. *either to Charles Brandons . . . the Nation affords: they be all three*] 1676 *has instead*: "either to Mr. Margrave, who dwells amongst the booksellers in St. Paul's Churchyard, or to Mr. John Stubs, near to the Swan in Golding Lane: they be both. . . ."

P. 236, l. 16. *Charls Brandons*] 1676 *has*: ". . . . . ."

P. 237, l. 14. *baited with it*] 1676 *adds*: "And you may also note, that the spawn of most fish is a very

tempting bait, being a little hardened on a warm tile
and cut into fit pieces. Nay, mulberries, and those
blackberries which grow upon briers, be good baits for
Chubs or Carps: with these many have been taken in
ponds, and in some rivers where such trees have grown
near the water, and the fruit customarily dropped into
it. And there be a hundred other baits, more than can
be well named, which, by constant baiting the water,
will become a tempting bait for any fish in it."

P. 239, l. 15. *a hole*] 1676 *has*: "any great still hole.
. . ."

P. 239, l. 24. *be cleft*] 1676 *has*: "be a little hazel or
willow cleft. . . ."

CHAPTER XVIII

P. 242, l. 1. *taken out*] 1676 *adds*: "and not washed
after. . . ."

P. 242, l. 4. *Tansie*] 1676 *adds*: "thus used they make
a dainty dish of meat."

P. 243, l. 9. *Summer birds*] 1676 *has*: "half-year
birds. . . ."

CHAPTER XIX

P. 248, l. 3. *one*] 1676 *has*: "one strange fish. . . ."

P. 248, l. 25. *strange Beasts*] 1676 *has*: "such strange
fish and beasts. . . ."

CHAPTER XX

P. 251, l. 5. *Tench*] 1676 *adds*: "when 'tis left to the
mercy of ducks or vermin."

P. 252, l. 4. *moneths*] 1676 *adds*: "if the pond be clean."

CHAPTER XXI

P. 255, l. 9-10. *not break . . . all together*] 1676 *has*: "break altogether, which hairs of an unequal bigness never do, but break singly, and so deceive the angler that trusts to them."

P. 257, l. 13. *lay on a second*] 1676 *adds*: "Well, scholar, having now taught you to paint your rod, and we having still a mile to Tottenham High Cross, I will, as we walk towards it, in the cool shade of this sweet honeysuckle hedge, mention to you some of the thoughts and joys that have possessed my soul since we two met together. And these thoughts shall be told you, that you also may join with me in thankfulness to the Giver of every good and perfect gift, for our happiness. And that our present happiness may appear to be the greater, and we the more thankful for it, I will beg you to consider with me, how many do, even at this very time, lie under the torment of the stone, the gout, the toothache; and this we are free from. And every misery that I miss is a new mercy; and therefore let us be thankful. There have been, since we met, others that have met disasters of broken limbs; some have been blasted, others thunderstrucken: and we have been freed from these, and all those many other miseries that threaten human nature; let us therefore rejoice and be thankful. Nay, which is a far greater mercy, we are free from the unsupportable burthen of an accusing, tormenting conscience; a misery that none can bear: and therefore let us praise Him for His preventing grace, and say, Every misery that I miss is a new mercy. Nay, let me tell you, there be many that have forty times our estates, that would give the greatest part of it to be healthful and cheerful like us; who, with the expense of a little money, have eat and drank, and laughed, and angled, and sung, and slept securely; and rose next day and cast away care, and sung, and laughed, and angled again; which are blessings rich men cannot purchase with all their money. Let me tell you, scholar, I have a rich neighbour that is always so busy that he has no leisure to laugh; the whole business of his life is to get money, and more money, that he may still get more and more money; he is still drudging on, and says, that Solomon says, 'The diligent hand maketh rich;' and 'tis true indeed: but he considers not that 'tis not in the power of riches to make a man happy: for it was wisely said, by a man of great observation, that there be as many miseries beyond riches as on this side them. And yet God deliver us from pinching poverty; and grant, that having a competency, we may be content and thankful. Let not us repine, or so much as think the gifts of God unequally dealt, if we see another abound with riches; when, as God knows, the cares that are the keys that keep those riches hang often so heavily at the rich man's girdle, that they clog him with weary days and restless nights, even when others sleep quietly. We see but the outside of the rich man's happiness: few consider him to be like the silk-worm, that, when she seems to play, is, at the very same time, spinning her own bowels, and consuming herself. And this many rich men do, loading themselves with corroding cares, to keep what they have, probably, unconscionably got. Let us therefore be thankful for health and a competence; and above all, for a quiet conscience.

"Let me tell you, scholar, that Diogenes walked on a day, with his friend, to see a country fair; where he saw ribbons, and looking-glasses, and nut-crackers, and fiddles, and hobby-horses, and many other gim-cracks; and, having observed them, and all the other finnimbruns that make a complete country-fair, he said to his friend, 'Lord, how many things are there in this world of which Diogenes hath no need!' And truly it is so, or might be so, with very many who vex and toil themselves to get what they have no need of. Can any man charge God, that He hath not given him enough to make his life happy? No, doubtless; for nature is content with a little. And yet you shall hardly meet with a man that complains not of some want; though he indeed wants nothing but his will; it may be, nothing but his will of his poor neighbour, for not worshipping, or not flattering him; and thus, when we might be happy and quiet, we create trouble to our-selves. I have heard of a man that was angry with him-self because he was no taller; and of a woman that broke her looking-glass because it would not show her face to be as young and handsome as her next neighbour's was. And I knew another to whom God had given health and plenty; but a wife that nature had made peevish, and her husband's riches had made purse-proud; and must, because she was rich, and for no other virtue, sit in the highest pew in the church; which being denied her, she engaged her husband into a contention for it, and at last into a law-suit with a dogged neighbour who was as rich as he, and had a wife as peevish and purse-proud as the other: and this law-suit begot higher oppositions, and actionable words, and more vexations and law-suits; for you must remember that both were rich and must therefore have their wills. Well, this wilful, purse-proud law-suit lasted during the life of the first husband; after which his wife vexed and chid, and chid and vexed, till she also chid and vexed herself into her grave: and so the wealth of these poor rich people was cursed into a punishment, because they wanted meek and thankful hearts; for those only can make us happy. I knew a man that had health and riches; and several houses all beautiful and ready furnished, and would often trouble himself and family to be removing from one house to another; and being asked by a friend why he removed so often from one house to another, replied, It was to find content in some one of them. But his friend, knowing his temper, told him, If he would find content in any of his houses, he must leave himself behind him; for content will never dwell but in a meek and quiet soul. And this may appear, if we read and consider what our Saviour says in St. Matthew's Gospel; for He there says: 'Blessed be the merciful, for they shall obtain mercy. Blessed be the pure in heart, for they shall see God. Blessed be the poor in spirit, for theirs is the kingdom of heaven.' And—'Blessed be the meek, for they shall possess the earth.' Not that the meek shall not also obtain mercy, and see God, and be comforted, and at last come to the kingdom of heaven: but in the meantime, he, and he only, possesses the earth, as he goes toward that kingdom of heaven, by being humble and cheerful, and content with what his good God has allotted him. He has no turbulent, repining, vexatious thoughts that he deserves better; nor is vexed when he sees others possessed of more honour or more riches than his wise God has allotted for his share: but he possesses what he has with a meek and contented quietness, such a quietness as makes his very dreams pleasing both to God and himself.

"My honest scholar, all this is told to incline you to thankfulness; and to incline you the more, let me tell you, that though the prophet David was guilty of murder and adultery, and many other of the most deadly sins, yet he was said to be a man after God's own heart, because he abounded more with thankfulness than any other that is mentioned in Holy Scripture, as may appear in his Book of Psalms; where there is such a commixture of his confessing of his sins and unworthiness, and such thankfulness for God's pardon and mercies, as did make him to be accounted, even by God Himself, to be a man after His own heart: and let us, in that, labour to be as like him as we can; let not the blessings we receive daily from God make us not to value, or not praise Him because they be common; let not us forget to praise Him for the innocent mirth and pleasure we have met with since we met together. What would a blind man give to see the pleasant rivers, and meadows, and flowers, and fountains, that we have met with since we met together? I have been told, that if a man that was born blind could obtain to have his sight for but only one hour during his whole life, and should, at the first opening of his eyes, fix his sight upon the sun when it was in his full glory, either at the rising or setting of it, he would be so transported and amazed, and so admire the glory of it, that he would not willingly turn his eyes from that first ravishing object, to behold all the other various beauties this world could present to him. And this, and many other like blessings, we enjoy daily. And for most of them, because they be so common, most men forget to pay their praises: but let not us; because it is a sacrifice so pleasing to him that made that sun and us, and still protects us, and gives us flowers, and showers, and stomachs, and meat, and content, and leisure to go afishing.

"Well, scholar, I have almost tired myself, and, I fear, more than almost tired you. But I now see Tottenham High Cross; and our short walk thither shall put a period to my too long discourse; in which my meaning was, and is, to plant that in your mind with which I labour to possess my own soul; that is, a meek and thankful heart. And to that end I have showed you, that riches without them do not make any man happy. But let me tell you, that riches with them remove many fears and cares. And therefore my advice is, that you endeavour to be honestly rich, or contentedly poor: but be sure that your riches be justly got, or you spoil all. For it is well said by Caussin, 'He that loses his conscience has nothing left that is worth keeping.' Therefore be sure you look to that. And, in the next place, look to your health: and if you have it, praise God, and value it next to a good conscience; for health is the second blessing that we mortals are capable of; a blessing that money cannot buy; and therefore value it, and be thankful for it. As for money, which may be said to be the third blessing, neglect it not: but note, that there is no necessity of being rich; for I told you there be as many miseries beyond riches, as on this side them: and if you have a competence, enjoy it with a meek, cheerful, thankful heart. I will tell you, scholar, I have heard a grave divine say, that God has two dwellings, one in heaven, and the other in a meek and thankful heart. Which Almighty God grant to me, and to my honest scholar: and so you are welcome to Tottenham High Cross."

P. 257, l. 14-19. *Well, Scholar . . . I will*] 1676 *has instead*:

"VENATOR. Well, master, I thank you for all your good directions; but for none more than this last, of thankfulness, which I hope I shall never forget. And pray let's now rest ourselves in this sweet shady arbour, which nature herself has woven with her own fine fingers; 'tis such a contexture of woodbines, sweet-briar, jessamine, and myrtle; and so interwoven, as will secure us both from the sun's violent heat, and from the approaching shower. And being set down will. . . ."

P. 262, l. 22. *rested themselves from*] 1676 *has*: "rested and enjoyed themselves free from. . . ."

P. 264, l. 3-4. *and all that love to be quiet*] 1676 *has instead*: "and dare trust in His providence; and he quiet. . . ."